THE CHURCH THEN AND NOW

THE CHURCH THEN AND NOW
Cultivating a Sense of Tradition

Dr. William A. Scott
Frances M. Scott

Leaven Press
Kansas City, Mo.

Leaven Press is a service of National Catholic Reporter
Publishing Inc.

Library of Congress Catalog Card Number: 84-52876

ISBN: 0-934134-30-8

Published by:
Leaven Press
P.O. Box 40292
Kansas City, MO 64141

Printed and bound in the United States of America

CONTENTS

Introduction

Understanding the meaning of scripture in light of contemporary biblical scholarship and an awareness of the effect that history has had on the church's life are the foundations of today's Christian self-understanding. The past several decades have produced a revolution in our understanding of scriptuure and a dramatically expanded ability to trace the influence history has had in shaping the belief, the structure and the worship of the Roman Catholic church. The consequence of these developments has been the emergence of a quite new image of what it means to be Christian.

Of the two developments — understanding scripture and an awareness of history — the second is more fundamental. Building a Christian self-identity starts with a sense of history, a realization that the books embodying our beliefs and the lives that have been lived in consequence of those beliefs are both products of historical environment. Men who embodied the history of their times wrote Christianity's sacred books; people set in specific historical situations lived out the implications of those books in the midst of the events that shaped their lives. To know Christianity is to know its history. Or, as Teilhard de Chardin put it: "Everything is the sum of its past and nothing is comprehensible except through its history." The purpose of this book is to develop a sense of history, an awareness that Christianity's belief and practice have been shaped by the historical events of the centuries of its existence.

1

Creating a new Christian identity can be a painful and threatening experience bringing with it both guilt and fear. The problem is all the more threatening and disturbing for Roman Catholic Christians who have grown up believing that their form of Christianity was the only form. "Christian truth and Catholic life are changeless," has been the bedrock on which their faith rested. One way, perhaps the only way, to deal with the problem is to acquire a sense of history, an awareness that history has shaped the form of Christianity through all its centuries. Put another way, change in response to historical circumstances has characterized Christianity from its beginning. The notion that the church is changeless is of relatively recent origin. It came about because Christians lost a sense of their history and the change that characterized their history.

At a particular point in that history, the 16th century, some members found serious problems with the then existing form of the church. In protest, they left her to develop what seemed to them a more scriptural form of church. Faced with this challenge, the leadership of the church convened in council, the Council of Trent (1545-1563). It fashioned a defense of the form under attack by the reformers and established it as the only authentic form of the Christian church. For four centuries the full power of the church's leadership was given to defending and perpetuating the form of church defined at Trent. Created to meet a particular historical crisis, the challenge of the Reformation, this counter-reformation church acquired the note of immutability, of changelessness, and succeeding generations of Roman Catholic Christians came to see the Tridentine church as the only form possible for the church.

Then in 1959, suddenly and unexpectedly, John XXIII announced his intention to call a council. In its opening sessions in 1962, the council made clear that it saw its task to be a reformulation of the life of the church, an attempt to develop a form of church more responsive to the contemporary world than the Tridentine model. The council documents were a blueprint, a set of sketches of what the new form of church might be. More than two decades later we are still implementing that blueprint. It is not yet clear whether the new form of church will be successful in replacing the form created at Trent.

A substantial number of Catholics are still committed to the view that the church is changeless. Suggesting the need for change and insisting that Christians must be open to answers other than the one given by Trent is for them tantamount to a betrayal of the Christian faith.

This book is written for those who see the Second Vatican Council as a watershed as well as for those who see it as a disaster. The hope is to give a sense of Christian history to both. The form of the church that Trent canonized four centuries ago may be changeless. However, an awareness of the life of the church during the 15 centuries preceding Trent provides abundant evidence that from its beginning the church has adjusted to and been shaped by the course of human events. These events have always formed the context of its existence. The changes have not always been good but they show that flexibility and adaptation are essential components of the church's life. Indeed, they are the final proof of its vitality. What is alive adapts and changes. Immobility, the inability to adjust and change, is a sign of death, not life.

Part I will look at the life of the church from the beginning to the 16th century, paying particular attention to the way history shaped three elements: organizational structure, liturgy and belief. Part II will study the crisis of the 16th century, the Protestant Reformation and the Council of Trent's response, the creation of the Counter-Reformation church, and will examine expressions of the Tridentine church during the four centuries from Trent to Vatican II:

opposition to the emerging modern world, the First Vatican Council, modernism and the papacy from Pius IX to Pius XII. Part III will consider the blueprint for a new form of church produced by Vatican II and trace the lines of development since the council.

PART I:

From the Beginning to the 16th Century

Chapter 1

Organization and Structure — Ministry and Leadership

In the beginning, ministry and leadership in the church developed in response to need. The initial need was for the gospel to be preached. To meet that need Jesus had chosen the Twelve and given them a leader, Peter. In addition, other itinerant preachers of the Christian message, such as Paul, traveled from town to town establishing Christian communities. In the early years this latter group, together with the Twelve, were known as apostles — those sent to preach. But by the time the gospels were written the term apostle had come to be applied only to the original Twelve companions of Jesus. (This is especially true in Luke's gospel.) The New Testament makes clear these two groups gave themselves to preaching the good news as their primary ministry.

The Acts of the Apostles tells us of the next development. As the believers grew, some in the community — the widows, the poor, the orphans — needed food and shelter. Recognizing this the community chose from their number ministers to take care of these needs. Thus the order of deacon was born.

The next stage in the developing organization of the church occurred as Paul and other preachers traveled spreading the gospel to the gentile world. In each town he visited Paul would stay for several months winning converts by preaching and establishing a Christian community. His work of founding a church completed, Paul moved on to the next town but before leaving he gave each community its own leadership to care for its needs. He chose a group of men, the elders or presbyters, whose ministry was to preach, to teach and to lead the celebration of the Lord's Supper. Gradually, as these local churches grew, they came to see the need for a single leader to act as their spokesman with the other churches, and to serve as center and symbol of their unity. One of the elders was chosen to be leader of the local community. He became the overseer, the *episcopus,* the bishop of the Christian community. Chosen by the community, he was given the responsibility and the power to lead. He alone preached, led the eucharistic celebration, taught, and administered the sacraments. Of all his ministries, his primary one was to preach and teach the word of God.

By the middle of the second century, this had become the organizational structure of the church: Each local community had its own bishop, his assistants and advisors, the presbyters and the deacons, to care for the poor. The bishop alone led public worship and preached. His right-hand men in serving the needs of his community were the deacons. They played an active role in the liturgy — distributing eucharist, reading the scriptures and leading the community in prayer. They were also responsible for serving the needs of the poor and thus had care of church finances.

During the early centuries other ministries of service emerged as need arose. Men in the community took on these ministries, originally as a lifetime commitment. To care for the church and its furnishings the order of porter developed. Acolytes were chosen to assist the bishop in the eucharistic celebration. The reading of the scriptures at the liturgy was entrusted to the lectors. And, as the process of admitting new members to the community became more formal and more organized, a group known as exorcists came to play an important role in preparing members.

Until about 350 A.D., Christianity was principally confined to the towns and this organizational structure was sufficient to serve the needs of the churches. In the early 4th century, Constantine granted Christianity the legal right to exist. As a result, the Christian church experienced a period of rapid growth and began to spread into the rural areas. No longer able to serve the needs of an expanding church, the bishops began to turn over the care of churches in the outlying communities to their assistants, the presbyters. For these churches, the presbyters, or priests, began to exercise the same functions as the bishops performed in the towns. Thus the presbyters or priests gradually replaced the bishop as the leader of the local Christian community. As this occurred, the other ministries that had grown up diminished in importance. Eventually the orders of porter, lector, acolyte, exorcist and deacon, once taken on as lifetime commitments, became temporary stepping stones on the way to priesthood.

In these early centuries, in which need and historical circumstances shaped the ministries in the church, teaching and ruling authority were undergoing a similar evolution. To begin with each local church was autonomous, subject to the teaching and ruling authority of its own, community-chosen bishop. He was seen as successor of the apostles and thus possessing their authority over his church. The growth and spread of Christianity brought questions of belief and practice that affected all the churches of an area. The bishops of the area began to meet to deal with questions of faith, problems of discipline, and matters regarding liturgical worship. Their meetings, originally informal, gradually were formalized into synods that met regularly to decide matters affecting their churches and their decisions were accepted as normative by the commmunities they led. For questions affecting the entire Christian church, particularly matters of doctrine, the bishops came together in general council and their teachings were seen as an expression of authentic and apostolic authority. Thus leadership in the first several hundred years was exercised by the bishops meeting in groups to regulate the life and the belief of the Christian churches. It was a shared or collegial exercise of teaching and ruling authority.

The ministers in the church during the first centuries did not constitute a group set apart. Like other community members, they married, raised families and earned their living at a full-time job. Their life-style did not differ significantly from that of their fellow Christians. But as the churches grew and the demands of ministry multiplied, congregations undertook to support their ministers and they gradually withdrew from secular work to give themselves fully to the service of the community.

At the same time this movement to full-time ministry was occurring, the understanding of Christian priesthood was undergoing a change. At first the presbyters or elders saw their primary ministry as preaching and teaching the word of God. They did not see themselves nor were they seen by their communities as the Christian counterparts of the Jewish or pagan "priesthoods, whose principal function was liturgical — offering sacrifice and leading the faithful in worship. But then came a shift in the church's teaching from emphasizing the humanity of Jesus to emphasizing his divinity. Denials of the divinity of Jesus in the fourth and succeeding centuries brought about this shift. It produced a change in the way the role of the presbyter was viewed. As priest he had the power to make Jesus the Lord present among the people in the eucharistic celebration. This was an awesome and sacred role. It came to be seen as incompatible with marriage and the begetting of children. The sacred character of the priesthood demanded celibacy. By the end of the fourth century the leaders of the church were insisting that priests be celibate.

The Rise of the Papacy

From the earliest days of Christianity the church of Rome held a place of special reverence and respect because Peter, the leader of the apostles, had been its first bishop. Rome was the capital of the empire and that added to the honor and prestige given its bishop. There is, however, no indication in the records coming down to us that the bishop of Rome in the first four centuries saw his position as giving him universal jurisdiction over the churches of Christianity. He was seen as Peter's successor and bishop of the capital city but there is no evidence that he claimed teaching and ruling authority over the whole Christian church. His fellow bishops, especially those who ruled as patriarchs over the great cities of the East — Jerusalem, Antioch, Alexandria — accorded him primacy by reason of their veneration for the see he occupied but it was a primacy of honor among equals. They also saw themselves as successors of the apostles and therefore as possessing the same apostolic authority as he.

Damasus (366-84) seems to have been the first to claim universal primacy over all the Christian churches. His successor, Daricius, made the same claim and began acting on the claim with doctrinal and disciplinary decrees that were directed to the universal church. This trend grew stronger under subsequent bishops of Rome. Finally, in the middle of the next century, historical circumstance and a man of exceptional ability came together to produce not merely the claim but the power and prestige needed to establish the bishop of Rome as the supreme ruler, teacher and judge of at least the western half of Christianity.

The historical circumstance was the gradual disintegration of the Roman empire under the pressure of the barbarian tribes seeking to expand their territory. As the empire fell apart the emperor moved his capital to Constantinople and a leadership vacuum developed in the West. The bishop of Rome filled this vacuum as the clergy and the laity looked increasingly to him for leadership, protection and material aid.

Into this historical situation stepped Leo I (440-461), a remarkably gifted and spiritual man. Leo carefully spelled out the papal claim. He saw the bishop of Rome, by virtue of being Peter's successor, as holding universal jurisdiction over the Christian churches. As he saw it, this authority was shared by the other bishops but subject to his primacy. The man and the moment established the Roman primacy.

Succeeding historical circumstances conspired to add their own strength to papal supremacy. The African church, whose bishops strongly resisted the Roman claim to universal jurisdiction, was swept away by the Moslem invasion. As a result, one voice challenging the papal claim was silenced. The influence of the bishops of eastern Christianity waned as the eastern half of the empire separated itself more and more from the West. Thus history itself removed resistance to Roman ascendancy.

The chaos and anarchy that marked the age of the barbarian invasions lasted over 300 years. During that period, the church of Rome began seeing its mission as converting the barbarians to the faith. Missionaries sent by Rome carried Christianity to Ireland and England. The faith they planted acknowledged Rome's primacy. From this Irish and English church monks crossed into Europe carrying the faith to the lands that are now France and Germany. As a result, the faith of the newly converted Franks and Saxons centered on Rome as well.

The final stage in establishing papal primacy was reached

as western Europe began emerging from chaos in the latter half of the eighth century. Pope Stephen, recognizing the emergence of the Frankish tribe as the military and political leader in the West, journeyed to Paris in 754 and anointed Pepin, their leader, as king. Pepin, in response, promised to protect the church of Rome and made Stephen a temporal ruler by giving him the papal states.

The climax of the re-establishment of the Roman empire, now the Holy Roman Empire, came when Pepin's son, Charlemagne, was crowned emperor by Pope Leo III in Rome on Christmas day, 800 A.D. The marriage of the Christian church under the leadership of the bishop of Rome and the civil state under the leadership of the emperor was solemnized.

The relationship between empire and church, emperor and pope, remained a good one for the hundred years that Charles' line ruled. But by the beginning of the 11th century the period of Carolingian rule ended. The empire passed into the hands of the Saxon kings, who were German emperors. They took control of the church, subjecting it to imperial policy. Otto I, in the middle of the century, imposed his will on the people of Rome. Until then the bishop of Rome had been chosen by the Roman clergy and laity. But Otto forced them to take an oath promising not to choose a bishop until he approved their choice. And, the bishop-elect could not accept until the emperor confirmed his election. In short, the choice of pope became the emperor's prerogative. He saw to it that the man chosen was his man and did his will. The result was that the papacy came under the absolute control of the empire. In consequence, a gradual secularization of the papal office began.

This situation continued for almost a hundred years until the papacy of Nicholas VI (1058-61). Recognizing that the child emperor (Henry IV) was powerless to block him, Nicholas changed the method for papal election. Henceforth, the pope would be chosen by the Roman cardinals. Control of the papacy passed from the hands of the emperor to the cardinals. Until Nicholas' decree the cardinals had been pastors of the great churches of Rome. Now they became electors of the leader of the Christian church.

The position of cardinal carried grave responsibility and enormous power. As long as their responsibility to serve the needs of the church universal was the cardinals' primary concern, the system worked well and their choices were made in the best interests of the church. Unfortunately over the next several centuries, they abused their power and that brought tragic consquences for the church. But before turning to that story we must look at another development in the organizational structure of the church.

In 1073 Gregory VII came to the papal throne. Like his predecessor Leo I, Gregory was an extraordinary man. He possessed exceptional adminstrative ability as well as being a man of strong will and deep spirituality. The secularization of the church brought on by the domination of the Saxon emperors cried out for reform. Gregory made that reform the principal task of his pontificate. For Gregory reform meant firm control by the bishop of Rome over the church and particularly its bishops. Through a series of measures Gregory centralized power in the church in the hands of the Roman pontiff. He himself appointed bishops, gave them advice and reprimand, did not hesitate to remove them and insisted that their true role in the church was to be found in union with and dependence on the pope. In this process of centralizing authority in the church, Gregory made the cardinals his principal administrative assistants. The cardinals — as a group known as the curia — became his advisers and collaborators in governing church.

With Gregory's reform, the strongly centralized medieval church began to take shape. At its head was the pope in Rome. With the assistance of his curia he administered a church that had become strongly Roman. It worshiped in a single rite, obeyed a common law and was united in close adherence to the rule of the papacy

This centralizing trend meant more power for the cardinals. As electors of the pope who ruled the Christian church, their power, prestige and wealth grew enormously through the 12th and succeeding centuries. The extraordinary power they wielded meant that they were for all practical purposes rulers of the universal church along with their head, the bishop of Rome. This group of powerful cardinals was rarely larger than 15 or 16 during most of the Middle Ages.

With the onset of the 13th century, the tragic abuse of power by the cardinals began. It became common practice for the cardinal electors to exact promises of future favors from the candidates being considered for the papal office. When they gathered in 1268 to choose a successor to Clement IV, they were unable to reach a decision for three years. Finally an enraged Roman mob cut off their food supply and tore the roof from their meeting place. Within a few days the cardinals chose a deacon to succeed Clement, but another half year passed before he was ordained and installed. Thus did 16 men deprive the Christian church of leadership for almost four years.

Next followed 75 years during which the papal court was moved from Rome to Avignon in southeastern France. Clement was Archbishop of Bordeaux when chosen pope. He did not relish the thought of residing in a Rome hostile to a pope who was not Italian. He chose to remain in France, setting up his papal court at Avignon. From 1305 to 1377 seven popes remained there finding their homeland a more congenial residence than Rome. Finally, in 1378 Gregory XI returned the papacy to Rome only to die there within the year. The stage was set for one of the great tragedies in the church's history. As the cardinals entered the conclave, the people of Rome made clear how unhappy they would be if the choice were not an Italian. They got what they wanted — an Italian, Urban VI. As pope, he began almost immediately to implement a series of measures aimed at reforming the college of cardinals. The cardinals reacted by announcing that fear of the Roman mob had heavily influenced their choice and thus it was invalid.

Retiring to Avignon, the cardinals held a second conclave and elected Robert of Geneva, a Frenchman, as Clement VII. Clement settled the papal court in Avignon again. Now there were two popes. The Great Western Schism had begun. Christians found themselves forced to choose between two papal claimants. The impasse lasted for 30 years until finally, in 1409, the cardinals attempted to end the scandal by convening a general council at Pisa. They deposed the Roman and the Avignon claimants and elected Alexander V. But none of the three recognized the claims of the others. The result was three popes.

Finally the emperor intervened, summoning a council at Constance (1414-1418). To break the power of the cardinals, representatives of the nation states were given the right to vote. All three claimants were deposed and Martin V was chosen pope. With his choice the schism ended but the scandal given by the church's leadership was long remembered. Within a hundred years, there would be those who would say it cast serious doubt on the Roman church's claim to be the church of Christ.

The Council of Constance made strong recommendations for reforming the small group of men who had caused such grave harm to the church but their power remained too great and the reform did not take place. The cardinals domination of the church and the papacy continued.

In the latter half of the 15th century, the cardinals' abuse of power moved to its next stage. The great families of Rome — the Borgias, the Colonnas, the Medici, the Della Rovoreo — came to dominate the curia and, in consequence, the papacy. The papal office was used shamelessly to confer ecclesiastical position and power on family members. Nephews of the reigning pontiffs became cardinals and were appointed bishops of the great dioceses of western Christianity. Again, there was no weapon strong enough to curtail the abuse.

Finally, Leo X (1513-1521) created 31 new cardinals, a group international in character, and at long last the power of the small group of cardinals was broken. But by then it was too late. It was the same Leo who excommunicated Martin Luther. The Protestant Reformation had begun. No small part of its protest was directed at the scandalous misuse of power by the leadership of the church.

The Council of Trent was convened in 1545 to purify and reform the church in answer to the challenge of the reformers. Its accomplishments were impressive. In response to Protestantism, it spelled out in careful detail the clements of Christian belief. In matters of discipline, it corrected many of the abuses that had beset the church for centuries. But the organizational structure of the church was left intact. Roman Catholicism emerged from the council as a strongly centralized church with the pope exercising supreme teaching and ruling authority in a manner more absolute than at any point in its history. The Roman curia was reformed and purified of the abuses that had marred its administration of church affairs in recent centuries. The college of cardinals, however, continued to exercise central power in governing the church for another 400 years.

Not until the second Vatican Council (1962-65) was the issue of the organizational structure of the church addressed again. That council raised the question: In what manner and by whom should teaching and ruling authority in the church be exercised? The answer it suggested differed from the answer of Trent. We will leave the details of that answer until we discuss the Second Vatican Council in Part III.

Chapter 2

The Worship and Piety of the Church

We are tracing the effect history had on elements of the church's life from its beginning to the 16th century. In Chapter One, we traced the transformation of the organizational structure. Leadership and authority vested in the bishops in the early centuries was passed on in later centuries to the papacy and the college of cardinals.

We turn now to examine history's effect during the first 1,600 years on a second element of the church's life — worship and piety. Christian worship is rooted in the Last Supper. What Jesus did at that final meal was the basis of the primitive church's liturgy. The first Christians came together to repeat and to celebrate that supper, to do again what Jesus did the night before he died.

Four elements were emphasized in their celebration. First, they saw it was a *meal* at which they ate the bread of life, his body. Eating that bread united them with their Risen Lord and gave them his life. Second, they saw what they did as a *sacrifice*. They were making present again the body broken for them, the blood shed for them — the sacrifice that had won for them forgiveness of their sins and reconciliation with the Father. Third, they saw this eating and drinking together as the *cause of their union with one another*. In sharing the same meal, they shared the life that meal gave to all of them. By eating and drinking, they were united into a community, into one body. In that union, they expressed the love that they had for one another. Finally, they saw it as a *eucharist, a thanksgiving*. It was the occasion to recall and be thankful for what Jesus had done for them. It was the moment for joyful celebration of God's goodness to his people.

Thus, at its beginning the church's worship was *simple* — a meal together recalling and celebrating the sacrifice of their Lord. And it was *communal* — all understood what was being done and all participated in the act of eating and recalling and celebrating.

Then history began to go to work on this simple, communal celebration, changing it over the centuries into a mysterious drama understood and performed only by the priest while the faithful stood by silent and uncomprehending. How and why did this happen? The answer lies in historical development.

First, there is *language*. In the apostolic age, the language of the people and hence of the eucharistic celebration was Greek. By the late 4th century, Latin had replaced Greek as the common language. Latin also was used in the church's worship because understanding the language facilitated communal participation, the heart of the liturgy.

In subsequent centuries (400-750), the Roman empire disintegrated and its place was taken by the barbarian tribes of Western Europe. Latin was no longer the language of the people, but other reasons had developed for retaining it as the official language of the church and of her worship. Over the centuries, Latin had become the traditional language of the church and traditions do not easily change. Furthermore, as the new empire of the west emerged it saw itself as replacing and continuing the revered Roman empire. As a result, establishing links with the venerable and treasured past was important. Latin had been the language of Rome; it was retained as the language of church, which tied the new empire to the old one. Finally, by the eighth century, the text of the mass had taken on a sacred character. Because of that, it had to be carefully guarded from translation into the rude, vulgar languages of the newly Christianized barbarians.

For these reasons, the liturgy passed out of the hands of the community into the hands of the priest, the only one who understood the language of worship. Emphasis in the liturgy passed from understanding to mystery. The focus of the eucharistic celebration moved from the community to the priest. In addition to leading the community, he became the mediator who spoke in an unintelligible tongue to God on behalf of the uncomprehending faithful. The communal link, with all participating, was lost.

Secondly, there is *altar*. For early Christianity the altar was the place of sacrifice and the table for the meal. Around it the community, priest and people, gathered to celebrate the sacrificial supper of their Lord. It was a plain, unadorned table/altar with no tabernacle, no candles, no crucifix — nothing to distract from the central action of making the Lord present again and eating the bread of life together. Its place, in the center of the community, and its function, the table of the supper and the altar of the sacrifice, underlined the understanding that the faithful had of their eucharistic celebration.

This simplicity and communality lasted for the first several hundred years while the church was a persecuted minority in the empire. In the fourth century, Christianity was given the right to legal existence. It also became the official religion of the empire. Inevitably, this new status brought with it a church architecture designed to reflect the importance of the church's position in society. Large and richly decorated edifices became the visible expressions of this importance. In these large structures, the altar lost its central position. Moved to the back wall, the altar tended to become but a part of their interior richness.

By the Middle Ages — perhaps most strikingly expressed in the magnificent Gothic cathedrals — the altar positioned against the back wall, had become more of a stage on which the priest acted out a sacred and mysterious drama than the table of the Lord around which his believing community gathered. Another link in the chain that bound the community together had been broken. A remote spectacle in an unknown tongue had replaced the communally shared banquet of the Lord.

The next change effected by historical circumstances was perhaps the most damaging to the community dimension of the eucharistic celebration. The early church had strong memories of the earthly life of Jesus. Remembering, they had a warm, very personal relationship to the eucharist where Jesus, their Risen Lord but human like them, came among his people. They celebrated that presence by eating his body and drinking his blood. It was unthinkable to be part of the community and not participate in its action — receiving the Lord. Everyone received gladly, gratefully; everyone celebrated the Lord's presence among them.

As the Christian church moved into the 4th and 5th centuries, some members began to ask disturbing questions about Jesus: was he really God or was he only God's representative, a man sent by God? As the questions multiplied, the church found it necessary to answer by insisting it had always believed Jesus was God's son, that he was equal of the Father, that he was God. As those who questioned the divinity of Jesus became more insistent, the church's response became firmer.

Yet another historical development added weight to this insistence on the divinity of Jesus. As the Roman empire crumbled and the barbarian tribes overran western Europe, the Christian church came to see that her future lay in the conversion of these tribes to Christianity. Thus in the fifth and succeeding centuries the missionary activity of the church was concentrated on winning the Visigoths, the Saxons and the Franks to the Christian faith. Many of the tribes had already accepted Christianity in its Arian form, a form of belief that saw Jesus as not divine but a creature subordinate to God. Converting them to the orthodox Christian faith demanded a heavy emphasis on the divinity of Jesus.

The consequence of this series of historical circumstances was that the doctrinal teaching of the church for many centuries focused strongly on the fact that Jesus was a divine person, co-equal with God the Father. That Jesus was a man, a human like us, was never denied but historical circumstances required insistence on his divinity.

The emphasis had its effect on the way the faithful related to the eucharist. As the humanity of Jesus receded in the church's consciousness and the stress on Jesus' divinity became ever more pronounced, people's attitude toward the eucharist underwent a dramatic change. If the bread and wine of the eucharist were indeed the very body and blood of God himself, then how could poor, sinful humans dare to presume to approach the altar and eat that body and drink that blood? The bread of life that all ate became the awesome, to-be-adored body of God. This attitude became so strong that by the Middle Ages it was rare for anyone to dare to receive communion. Unworthy humans did not dream of eating God's body. Adoration and reverence became the faithful's response to the eucharist. The situation became so bad that in the 13th century the church introduced a law requiring all Christians to receive the eucharist at least once a year. Thus was the Easter duty born. Again, the pressure of history had transformed the relationship of the faithful to the eucharist.

As a result, by the early middle ages a variety of devotions signaled a new era in eucharistic piety — devotion to Jesus really present in the eucharist. Toward the end of the 11th century a monk named Berengerius denied the real presence. The consecrated bread and wine, he maintained, were only symbols of Jesus. In response to this heresy, the monks at Cluny, one of the great monasteries of Europe, began to elevate the species at mass after the consecration to give the faithful the opportunity to adore Christ in the eucharist. The practice spread and within a hundred years it had become common in the western Christian church. The practice endured for nine centuries until the liturgical changes of the second Vatican Council.

Following the 11th century, the consecrated bread, the body of Jesus who was divine, became the object of the adoration and worship of the faithful. Ever more frequent opportunities to adore Jesus really present in the eucharist were created. A vessel of precious metal suitable for holding the sacred species, the monstrance, was devised. This was followed by the rise of benediction of the Blessed Sacrament, a new religious rite that became central in the cult of the real presence. Other opportunities to adore Jesus in the eucharist emerged: processions of the Blessed Sacrament on great feastdays, and its "exposition" for extended periods. Ultimately, the tabernacle appeared on altars. In it the consecrated body of Christ was reserved, offering uninterrupted opportunity to worship and adore our Lord present in the eucharist.

The cult of the real presence became central in the eucharistic life and piety of the church and for hundreds of years the interior life of the faithful was nourished by this devotion. For a long time many people found adoring Jesus in the eucharist more meaningful than receiving the bread of life. Gazing with reverential awe on the host, elevated or exposed, or visiting the Blessed Sacrament became the normal response of the faithful to the eucharist. Communal sharing in the meal/sacrifice, characteristic of the eucharistic life of the early centuries, all but disappeared History had indeed transformed the way Christians related to Jesus their Lord and Savior.

Two further transformations wrought by history in the understanding and celebration of the eucharist should be mentioned. First, there was a shift in the way the faithful related to the eucharist as a sacrifice. The early church saw its eucharistic celebration as a sacrifice. Community members knew they were making present again the one sacrifice that had won them pardon and reconciliation. The Lord's body, which had been broken for them, and the Lord's blood, which had been shed for them, were again present among his people. This was cause for joy and for celebration because the body and the blood had brought them redemption.

With the passage of time came the loss of an understandable language and the community lost awareness of what it was doing. As a result, only the priest offered sacrifice. The communal understanding of the eucharistic sacrifice was lost. Those same centuries that produced loss of a communally shared eucharistic language brought with them, as we have seen, a shift in emphasis from the humanity of Jesus to his divinity. A quite different perception of the meaning of the eucharistic sacrifice resulted. Because it was offered by Jesus who was divine, this sacrifice came to be seen as having infinite value. Through it, sinful humans could ask for and be confident of receiving the answer to all their needs and the needs, too, of their deceased relatives and friends. The idea of one altar and one sacrifice offered by the one community for all its needs vanished. In its place came private masses offered for private intentions. Altars and priests to say mass at those altars multiplied. Since saying mass became in many cases the only way a priest could support himself, the custom of making an offering for a mass celebrated for one's private intention arose. This attachment of money to mass provided ample opportunity for misunderstanding and misuse.

There was a second development over the centuries we are considering. As the two simple ideas of the eucharist as meal and as sacrifice faded and the community's active part in the eucharistic celebration disappeared, a vacuum was created. Now that the priest was the sole active participant in the eucharistic liturgy the people were left without meaningful involvement in the mass. There was a need to provide the faithful with fruitful ways of attending an otherwise unintelligible ritual. One way to meet this need was seeing the mass as a sacred mystery play or drama rich in all sorts of syumbolic meaning. Each gesture, each act, each element of the mass was made to yield its own meaning to feed the piety of the faithful.

The priest washing his hands recalled Pilate washing his hands of the innocent blood of Jesus; the cincture around the priest's waist represented the rope around Jesus' waist as he was dragged through the streets of Jerusalem to Calvary; the movement of the mass book from one side of the altar to the other signified the passage from the Old Testament of fulfillment. Water, wine, bread, candles, vestments and incense all were parts of a holy drama and all yielded prayerful meaning to the eye able to read their message. Layer after layer of symbolic interpretation was developed to make attendance at mass a meaningful experience for the silent, onlooking faithful. Again the focus was on private, personal participation in the mass and yet another obstacle was placed between the Christian community and the active involvement in the meal and the sacrifice that had once been theirs.

By the 15th century, some realized that communal celebration of the eucharist had all but disappeared from the church. The call for reform began. Three general councils of the church were held in the 15th and early 16th centuries (Constance 1414-1418, Florence 1431-1445, and Lateran V, 1512-1517) but each had its immediate and pressing problems and little was done to reform the liturgy.

Lateran V ended in March 1517. Seven months later at the end of October Luther posted his 95 theses and the events that would bring the tragic division of Christianity were set in motion. Reform for Luther meant, first of all, a biblical revolution. For him only in the scripture does one find God's word. Only belief in God's word as found in scripture brought salvation. If faith was so essential then God's word, the scripture, in which the object of faith was found, should be available to the believing community. Therefore, a vernacular Bible was needed. Luther met that need by translating the whole of the Old and New Testament into German.

Luther's reform was also a liturgical revolution. The eucharistic liturgy was the place where the word of God was to be heard and responded to in faith. "The principal purpose of any service of worship," Luther said, "is teaching and preaching the word of God." Because the faithful could respond in faith to God's offer of salvation only if they understood, the liturgy was put into the language of the people.

Luther and his fellow reformers introduced many of the needed liturgical reforms: The Bible and liturgy were put into an understandable language; the eucharistic celebration was structured to actively involve the people; hymns were written for the congregation; the chalice was restored to the faithful — both bread and wine were received; and, finally, to describe what was taking place when eucharist was celebrated, the name "Lord's Supper" was restored. It had been early Christianity's name for its communal meal/

sacrifice but the term had fallen into disuse and replaced by the word "mass" as the common word for the central Christian worship service.

The Council of Trent was called to respond to the reformers' understanding of Christian belief and practice. It removed many of the abuses current in the church; it also gave a clear doctrinal explanation of many essential elements of the Christian faith: the sources of revelation, the nature of salvation, the number and meaning of the sacraments. But liturgy and the celebration of the eucharist were left largely untouched. The offering of sacrifice by the priest remained in a tongue unintelligible to the laity. The question of a liturgy in the language of the people was simply bypassed.

There is understandable historical reason for the omission. In the climate of the times, reform of the liturgy was not a realistic possibility for the bishops of Trent. Reforming the liturgy would have come uncomfortably close to admitting the rightness of aspects of the Reformation. As a result, the mass remained in Latin and closed to the understanding and active involvement of the community. The church had to wait 400 more years for needed reform in the eucharist and the mentality that had a seriously distorted view of the eucharist had four more centuries to harden.

Chapter 3

The Belief of the Church

As with the organizational structure and liturgical life, the Christian church found that its faith was shaped by history. In the early centuries, the faith of the Christian communities was rooted in the scripture and Christ was the primary focus of belief.

Scripture provided the bishops with the content and imagery for their sermons. The story of Lazarus raised from the dead offered opportunity to speak of the new life given to those who came to faith in Jesus. The man born blind to whom sight was given became the paradigm of the Christian whose faith brought a new vision of the meaning of life. Old and New Testament figures and events all spoke of God's loving care for his people. The words and deeds of Jesus pointed the way to a life of concern for others.

A long period of preparation was required of new Christians so they could become familiar with the Bible. Two to three years were spent steeping the new converts in the meaning of Christianity as portrayed in scripture. The eucharistic liturgy embodied the scriptural message in visual and spoken form. The Lord's Supper as the gospel writers spoke of it was celebrated again. God's word was read to the congregation and its meaning explained. Each word, each act memorialized and made present again scripture's recurrent theme: God has loved and cared for people all through their history; the life, death and resurrection of

Jesus is the climactic expression of that age-old love.

As belief was drawn from the Bible so too Christ was the central focus of that belief. The faith of those early centuries was a Christ-faith. Several themes were dominant. Each expressed an aspect of this Christ-centered belief.

1) *Death/resurrection*. The essential meaning of Jesus for the believer was found in his death/resurrection. He died for our sins; he rose that we might have his life. His death won pardon and reconciliation with the Father; his resurrection brought new life. These two events in the life of Jesus were at the heart of Christian faith. Neither was seen alone; neither was emphasized at the expense of the other. He did not die for us; he died/rose for us. Each eucharistic liturgy celebrated both events. His death was made present again in the re-offering of his sacrifice; the Risen Lord came to the believing community bringing it his life.

2) *Christ, priest and mediator*. As the community came together to celebrate eucharist the Risen Lord was present as its priest. In the person of the community's leader, Christ the one priest offered once again the one perfect sacrifice by which he had won for mankind reconciliation with the Father. Only he could offer that sacrifice of pardon and peace because only he possessed at one and the same time the humanity of those for whom he sought forgiveness and the divinity of the Father to whom he offered his life to win that forgiveness. He was the *one* mediator between people and God.

3) *Jesus, human and divine*. The faith of early Christianity was in Jesus, human and divine, a man yet one with the Father, by nature God yet like us. His humanity and his divinity were equally objects of Christian faith. The emphasis in expressing that belief tended to fall on his humanity. It was as man that he sacrificed his life; it was

the human nature he shared with mankind that enabled him to mediate its needs with the Father.

4) *The church as community.* Finally, the primitive Christian community saw itself as the body of Christ. There was the shared conviction that each believer, by reason of eating the bread of life, lived the life of the Risen Lord. That shared life bound Christians to one another in the bond of charity. Believers were Christians as a community, not as individuals. And Christianity expressed itself in care and concern for fellow Christians. The love for one another was indeed the sign by which others recognized them to be Christians.

Drawn from scripture, focused on Christ, celebrated in communal liturgy, embodied in a life of charity — such was the faith of early Christianity. Then in the thousand year stretch between the peace of Constantine (313 A.D.) and the late Middle Ages a series of historical developments transformed the faith of ancient Christianity. By the 14th century Christians were expressing their faith in ways quite different from those just described. A look at some of these developments will strengthen the sense of history we are cultivating.

1) *Language.* Perhaps the most far-reaching contribution to this shift in creedal expression took place in the area of language. Latin gradually ceased to be the language of the people, of priest and laity alike. Its place was taken by the languages of the tribes of western Europe. Latin continued, however, to be the language not only of the church's liturgy but the Bible as well. In consequence, the Bible became increasingly a closed book, inaccessible to the majority of the faithful, including the parish priest, the principal link between the people and the faith of the church. The Bible, the well-spring of the ancient faith, dried up as a source of belief. Biblical faith came to be replaced by faith drawn from other sources, particularly from the doctrinal formu-

lations produced by the general councils of the church during these centuries.

2) Beginning with the Council of Nicaea in 325 and continuing for several centuries, the doctrinal attention of the church was drawn to the divinity of Jesus Christ. Faced with serious challenges to the belief that Jesus was divine the church responded with a series of doctrinal statements strongly stressing that Jesus was God, co-equal with the Father. He was a divine person, possessing two natures, human and divine. Heresy required reaction and it took the form of accenting the divinity of Jesus. There were two other emphases in the teaching of those early councils. The first was on the doctrine of the Trinity: God is one in nature but triune in person, Father, Son and Holy Spirit. The second was on Mary and her place in Christian belief: Mary is the mother not of the man Jesus but of the divine person, God the Son who became man. All three of these emphases would have their effect on the belief and the piety of the Christian people.

First, during these centuries devotion to the Trinity grew in importance. Gradually, Sunday focused on that devotion. Sunday as the day to memorialize the death/resurrection of Jesus became in succeeding centuries the day for expressing belief in the Trinity. By the early Middle Ages the feast of the Trinity had become a feast of the universal church and the prefaces of the Sunday masses had become trinitarian. By the 13th century the Sunday liturgy focused on expressing belief in the triune God and the Trinity had taken over the place in Christian worship once occupied by Jesus Christ, true God and true man.

In a similar development, the emphasis on Christ's divinity changed the early stress on the humanity of Jesus. His role as priest and mediator gradually yielded to emphasizing his divinity and the effect of this shift was to produce different expressions of piety and belief among the faithful.

2) *Christ, mediator.* The faithful of the early church saw Jesus as a man like themselves. Because he shared their humanity they could approach him with confidence that he would understand their needs. Because he was God's Son those needs would be carried to his Father and they would be heard and answered by the Father. As the doctrinal expression of the faith emphasized his divinity, the humanity of Jesus, though never denied, tended to move off into the shadows and the faith and piety of the people turned toward seeing Jesus as divine. Adoration and worship became the proper attitudes of sinful humans toward Jesus who was divine. How could human beings dare to approach with their needs the Lord of creation, the one who would one day judge the living and the dead? Bereft of his humanity Christ could no longer be seen as mediator between human beings and God. Now he was co-equal with the Father, God himself.

Yet human need continued. Christians still needed someone to mediate their needs to God. What better person to perform this task than Mary whom the Council of Ephesus (431) had declared to be the mother of God? A son could refuse his mother nothing that she would ask of him. Mary moved into the position of mediator between her son, Jesus Christ and sinful mankind. Gradually she came to share this function with the saints. These holy men and women who had lived lives so pleasing to God were surely able to carry the petitions of humans to the throne of God. Thus when Jesus could no longer be seen by people as the unique mediator between them and the Father, Mary and the saints became our intercessors.

This new role for Mary had a profound effect on the devotional life of the church. Over the centuries devotions in her honor multiplied as Mary became in the eyes of the faithful their surest access to her Son. The rosary, novenas and masses in her honor, pilgrimages to her shrines, and books extolling her glories all reflected the central position that devotion to Mary came to occupy in the prayer of Christians.

Illustrative of the growing influence of Mary on the way the church expressed its faith is the process by which the liturgical year developed during these centuries. In the beginning the resurrection was the central mystery of the Christian faith. Annually the feast of Easter recalled and celebrated that mystery. Indeed each Sunday was a little Easter celebrating as it did the death/resurrection of Jesus. The liturgical year comprised the yearly celebration of this paschal mystery and of the events preceding and flowing from it: passion, death, resurrection, ascension and pentecost. Lent was the period of prayer and fasting to prepare worthily for the celebration of Easter.

The growing importance of Mary in Christian piety was reflected in the expansion of the liturgical calendar. In the early centuries, the paschal mystery, the death/resurrection of Jesus, was central; in succeeding centuries the focus shifted to the incarnational cycle, the conception and birth of Jesus. Christmas, the birthday of Mary's son, was the centerpiece of this cycle, preceded nine months previously by the annunciation of the angel Gabriel to Mary that she would conceive and bear a son. The feast of Epiphany, commemorating the manifestation of this child to the Gentile nations, completed this cycle. And, finally, just as Lent was the period of preparation for Easter, Christmas acquired its period of preparation in the four weeks of Advent, recalling the 4,000 years of anticipation of the birth of the Savior. In this development, advent, which in the primitive church looked forward to the second coming of Jesus at the end of time, became in later centuries a looking back to the time of waiting for the first advent of Jesus.

The result of the shift in emphasis from death/resurrection to conception /birth has remained with the church for over a thousand years. In the piety and devotion of Christians, Christmas remains the central holyday of the year. In theory, Easter is the climax of the liturgical year; in practice, the baby in the manger is far more appealing to the devotional life of the faithful than are the empty tomb and the Risen Lord of Easter.

3)*The cross/crucifix.* One final illustration of the effect of history on faith and piety can be seen in the development of the cross/crucifix as a visible expression of faith in the Christian church. In the early ages of Christianity, the cross was the visible symbol of the meaning of Jesus. The cross spoke of sacrifice and death and visualized the passion and death of Jesus. Without a body, it also spoke of resurrection: he is not here. The empty cross preserved the scriptural understanding of Jesus; it said that the faith of the church was in Jesus dead/risen. Death and resurrection were equally objects of Christian faith.

In the next stage, the cross became the crucifix. Now Jesus was portrayed as present on the cross. But his presence was a regal, victorious one. The cross became the throne on which Jesus stood clad in kingly garments, his arms outstretched in a gesture of victory and invitation, the smile of victory on his face, the crown on his head a royal crown. Again, the presentation of the central mystery of the Christian faith reflected the scriptural understanding of that mystery: Jesus died/rose. Not the defeat of the cross but the victory of resurrection was the final meaning of Jesus.

The last stage in the development came as the Middle Ages were nearing their end. During the 14th and 15th centuries a mood of pessimism and a preoccupation with death pervaded Europe. It was brought on by the series of historical events that dominated the period. The Black

Death (1348) decimated the population of Europe. The Great Western Schism (1378-1417) divided Christians among three claimants to the papal throne. England and France fought the Hundred Years War (1339-1453). Constantinople fell to the Moslems (1453). All these events suggested the world was nearing an end. This mood found religious expression in both the art and the piety. The death of Jesus on the cross was portrayed with stark realism. The accent fell on Christ's terrible price of suffering and despair: the pain-racked body on the cross crowned with thorns that pierced the head and sent great gouts of blood running down the face, the rib cage distended in the death agony, the gaping wounds in side and hands and feet. All these spoke poignantly of the bitter passion brought on Jesus by the sins of mankind.

Now, the passion and death engaged the attention and attracted the piety of the faithful. Devotions sprang up which invited sorrowing contemplation of the suffering and death on the cross. Signing oneself with the sign of the cross became popular. It was a way of expressing one's belief in the death of Jesus as the source of mankind's salvation. Stations of the Cross, a new religious ritual in the church spelled out each step from the garden to Calvary, and enabled Christians to accompany Jesus on his way. The last of the stations pictured the burial of Jesus, a note of sad finality quite alien to the gospel narrative in which the defeat of death is swallowed up in the victory of resurrection. Devotion to the five wounds and the precious blood offered other avenues for entering into communion with his awful suffering. At this time, the passion plays appeared. Relics of the passion — the true cross, the thorns, the nails, the burial shroud and Veronica's veil — all were eagerly sought and reverently venerated by king and peasant alike.

History had had its effect in fashioning the faith and the

piety of Christians. Death/resurrection, defeat overcome, and the balanced scripturally rooted faith of early Christianity yielded to a faith focused on the death of Jesus, on the price paid for sin and on the need for sorrow and penance.

We have looked at three aspects of the church's life: her organizational structure, her liturgy, and her belief and the expression of that belief in the piety and devotion of the faithful. In all three cases, the intent was to catch a glimpse of the way in which history shaped the life of the church in the first 1,500 years. The glimpse, if caught, should produce a sense of history — the realization that belief and practice are always possessed and expressed in the context of time. One cannot stop the film of history at a single frame and say: This is the church. For these 15 centuries, there is no single form of the church. The church organized, worshiped and believed in a variety of forms. This conclusion is important as we turn in Part II to a study of the Council of Trent. In answer to the Protestant Reformation, Trent fashioned a form of church that became *the* form of church. The changing church became the changeless church.

PART II:

Reformation, Council of Trent and the Church until Vatican II

Chapter 4

The Reformation and the Council of Trent

By the 16th century, many Christians saw that a general reform of the church was desperately needed. Yet little was done until the advent of Luther and his fellow reformers. They began to preach and to implement an understanding of Christianity that sharply challenged the belief and the practice of the church of the time. Reformation was begun but by those who saw no hope of implementing it. They left the church in protest with an understanding of Christianity drawn solely from the pages of scripture.

The basic difference between the reformers and the Roman Catholic position centered on the nature of salvation. How is a person saved? Through personal experience Luther had come to the conviction he was a sinner. Because of that, he could not please God by what he did. If salvation depended on what people did, he concluded, they were certainly lost. Good works could not produce salvation because people were sinners and not capable of good works. His study of Paul led him to see that it is not what people did but what God does that brings salvation. Knowing people's inability to save themselves God sent his Son to bring them salvation. The message of the gospel is that God offers us salvation through the saving death of Jesus Christ. "In the gospel the justice of God is revealed," Paul had written. For Luther that meant God's answer to the problem of salvation was this: Since you are not able to save yourself

I will save you through Jesus Christ. To this divine offer
of salvation mankind's response needed to be: I believe that
God is at work in Jesus saving me. I accept God's offer of
salvation through Jesus.

Spelled out in theological language, Luther's experience
expressed the reformers' view of salvation in three short
phrases: *God alone saves.* Salvation is a gift, a grace from
God. God gives it. It is not because of what people do that
he gives it. It is unmerited, undeserved, unearned. As sinners, people cannot please God and thereby deserve his
love. God gives his love even though people are sinners and
undeserving of that love. *Faith alone saves.* The single contribution people make to their salvation is their belief, their
trust, their confidence that God saves them through Jesus
Christ. Like Abraham, Christians believe God when he
promises salvation. And their faith brings them salvation.
Scripture alone saves. There is only one source of saving
knowledge, only one place where God's plan for salvation
of mankind can be found and that is in God's word which
is the scripture. How is a person saved? The answer to that
question is to be found only in scripture.

Why were people incapable of doing anything to save
themselves? The answer lay in understanding the nature
of the original sin. As a result of that sin mankind's nature
was corrupted right down to its roots. As sinners, people
were incapable of doing good. They were inescapably sinners. Even after faith brings salvation they are still what
they are — sinners. But now they are graced with the merits
of Jesus Christ. And God sees them as so graced. At one
and the same time, they are sinner and saved. Because
they remain sinners, nothing they do contributes to their
salvation. It is solely and only the action of God that saves
them. Thus did the reformers firmly reject the notion that
people's good works in any sense affect their salvation. And
Luther had a ready answer to the claim — the letter of

James taught otherwise in a passage that said, "You must perceive that a person is justified by his works and not by faith alone." The letter was in Luther's view "a right strawy epistle" (or in modern parlance, not worth the paper [papyrus?] it was written on.)

According to Luther, the same scripture that answers the question of salvation also makes clear that the Roman Catholic church is wrong in its view of the sacraments. The New Testament speaks of only two sacraments as having been instituted by Christ. The other five are rituals added by the church. They were not instituted by Christ. Only Baptism and the Lord's Supper are clearly sacraments. The rest are not to be accepted.

To save mankind, Jesus offered the sacrifice of his life on the cross. Salvation was accomplished by that one all-sufficient sacrifice. Continuing to offer sacrifice, as the Roman church does in the mass, calls into question the sufficiency of the one perfect sacrifice of the cross. From this perspective, the mass as sacrifice is blasphemy. The Christian community should indeed come together to recall Christ's death on the cross, his sacrifice. But it is a recalling, a memorial service. And the primary purpose of this liturgical act is to offer opportunity for the word of God to be proclaimed. It affords an occasion for God's offer of salvation in Jeus Christ to be made again so the believing community may once more accept it.

Briefly, this is the rethinking of Christian belief as formulated by the reformers. The prime source of that formulation was scripture. Theirs was a scripturally rooted faith.

The Council of Trent was called to meet the challenge of Protestantism by explaining and defending the meaning of Christian revelation in response to the understanding adopted by the reformers.

Since the basic contention of the reformers was that the only true source for learning the Christian message was scripture, the bishops of Trent began their rejection of Protestantism by insisting that scripture and tradition have equal validity as sources of revelation. God's word was given to the church. From the beginning, the church's constant task was to interpret and explain the meaning of the scriptural message. The Bible was not sufficient; if the Bible was to be understood correctly, the divinely-assisted teaching authority of the church was also needed. Thus, there are two sources of revelation, scripture and tradition. One very fundamental difference between Catholicism and the Reformation was thus sharply drawn. Protestantism looked to the Bible as the sole source of revelation; Catholicism looked to the church and her teaching to learn the meaning of revelation. One was biblically oriented; the other church oriented.

Next, the fathers of Trent turned their attention to the nature of salvation. Recognizing that the understanding of salvation constituted the essential difference between Catholicism and Protestantism, the council spent a great deal of time during its first years spelling out the Catholic understanding of salvation in careful detail.

Luther's search for an answer to the question of how a person is saved led him to conclude that the answer given by the 16th century church differed from that of the New Testament, especially as understood in the writings of St. Paul. For Paul and for Luther, "the just man lives by faith." Faith in Jesus as savior brings salvation. The church, however, affirmed that people were saved by their faith and their good works.

For the reformers human nature was essentially corrupted by original sin. In consequence people were not able to be what God wants them to be. They could not perform good deeds. Only by accepting in faith God's offer to save them in Christ is it possible for them to be saved. To that salvation human beings contribute only their faith. In response, the council's view was that original sin wounded human nature but did not render it essentially evil. Yet, it remains true that, left to themselves, people are helpless. They cannot reach salvation on their own power. God, recognizing the powerlessness, sent his son to save mankind. Faith in Jesus as savior brings human beings salvation and gives them the power to overcome the wound in their nature. The saved are now able to be what God would have them be. In living the saved life (good works) people are making a positive contribution to their own salvation.

Trent's treatment of the sources of revelation and the nature of salvation made clear its answers to the reformers' three basic principles: *God alone saves,* but he will not save human beings without their cooperation; *faith alone saves,* but living faith expresses itself in good works; *scripture alone saves,* but the church's explanation of the meaning of scripture is needed if one is to understand the scriptural message rightly.

Aside from the question of salvation, the major focus of the council was the sacraments. Responding to the assertion that scripture speaks clearly of only two sacraments as instituted by Christ, the council said the church's continuing belief and practice from its beginning was that the celebration of seven sacraments was the clear will of its founder. In all three periods of the council (1545-47, 1551-52, 1562-63), a good deal of attention was given to sacramental doctrine: All seven of the sacraments were instituted by Christ; each conferred grace; each had a specific purpose.

The council gave particular attention to the eucharist as sacrament and as sacrifice because the reformers rejected important elements of the church's teaching on the subject. The eucharistic liturgy (the mass) was a *true sacrifice,* making present again the one all-sufficient sacrifice of the cross. It was not, as the reformers contended, merely a memorial service recalling that sacrifice. Further, Christ is really present in the *sacrament* of the eucharist. Various explanations of that presence proposed by Luther, Calvin and Zwingli were rejected. His presence is most correctly explained in terms of transubstantiation, a philosophical explanation of the nature of Christ's presence using the philosophy of Aristotle as interpreted by Thomas Aquinas.

The council's doctrinal decrees also dealt with other beliefs denied by the reformers, e.g., the existence of purgatory and the veneration of Mary and the saints, but the nature of salvation and of the sacraments represented the heart of its work and its view of the essential difference between the Catholic and the Protestant vision of Christianity.

The focus of Trent's work was on defending Catholic truth against the attack of the reformers. As a result, its teaching took a "countering" form. In effect, it said: You hold this to be the meaning of the Christian message; we, on the contrary, hold this to be its true meaning. Unfortunately, the nature of the crisis forced this way of speaking about Christian belief. It was an approach that of necessity stressed differences. It did not allow equal treatment for the elements of Christian faith (and they were considerable) that both parties accepted. The consequence has been that Protestantism and Catholicism have tended to express their possession of Christian truth in opposition to each other rather than in terms of a common Christian heritage with significant differences on salvation and sacrament.

The crisis Trent faced was real and threatening. Responding to that crisis occupied the council's full energy and attention. In consequence, church organization, liturgy and belief, whose development had created problems that called for attention, were left largely untouched by the council.

The organizational structure of the church, with power largely centralized in the pope and the cardinals of the curia, remained unchanged. Abuses were corrected and the system was renewed and purified but the system itself was left untouched. The question of the structure of the church would not be addressed until Vatican II.

In the liturgy the crying need was for a return to the language of the people in order to restore the communal dimension. The reformers seized the initiative in this area. They made the Bible central in their call for reform. Luther gave the people the Bible in their own tongue and fashioned a liturgy in a language they understood, a liturgy that focused on proclaiming and explaining the word of God. The response of the council to this initiative was to leave the question of a vernacular Bible or liturgy untouched. It simply did not treat the issue. The omission is understandable. For Trent to have produced or encouraged a vernacular Bible and liturgy would have come uncomfortably close to admitting the righteous of some aspects of the Reformation. Given the church of the times, this was not a realistic possibility.

The mass remained in Latin for another 400 years and thus remained inaccessible to the active participation of the community. Catholics produced an English version of the Bible within 50 years after the council (the Douay-Rheims version of 1582-1609) and again in the 18th century (the Challoner Revision of 1749-63). But for most Catholics the Bible remained a closed book until well into the 20th century. Their knowledge of the scripture came filtered through the teaching of the church. This teaching was expressed in the philosophical language of Trent and presented in the question and answer format of the catechism. The catechism replaced the scripture as the vehicle for communicating Christian belief.

Leaving the mass in Latin continued the importance of the priest. He was the active celebrant of the eucharistic liturgy. The church's central act of worship remained the exclusive domain of the clergy. This served two purposes. First, the reformers had denied that holy orders was a true sacrament. The celebration of the liturgy by the priest alone offered visual evidence of the centrality of his role, thereby asssuring the faithful that the ordained priesthood was an essential part of Catholicism. Second, Protestants moved toward developing an active role in the church for laymen. In doing so, they were challenging the right of the clergy to preempt all active roles in the church's life. One way for Trent to respond was to continue a Latin liturgy which guaranteed that the clergy's role would be the only active one in the church's worship.

The failure of Trent to respond to the need for a vernacular liturgy is understandable, given the challenge posed by the reformers. It remains, nonetheless, a tragedy that the liturgical reform so desperately needed to restore communal worship to the church was postponed for four more centuries.

In Part I, we looked at areas of the *church's belief* in Christ that were affected by the course of history. We saw how initial emphasis on Christ's humanity shifted to his divinity. In consequence, his role as priest and as mediator came to be undervalued. The unique mediator between God and mankind was replaced by the mediation of Mary and the saints. Our look at the late medieval development of devotion to the passion of Christ suggested it had replaced the early church's emphasis on the resurrection as an equally essential element of Christian belief. Lastly, we saw how the church lost her vision of herself as the body of Christ as the communal dimension of the liturgy disappeared.

Trent's decision not to deal with the vernacular, coupled with its choice of philosophical rather than biblical language, guaranteed the continuance of a Christian belief and practice lacking the early church's biblically rooted emphasis on Christ as mediator, the church as community, and the resurrection as the final meaning of Jesus. Four centuries were to pass before Pius XII would begin the restoration of these long neglected emphases to a central position in the consciousness of the church. His encyclical in 1943, *Divino Afflante Spiritu* mandated Catholic scholars to begin using the methods of scientific biblical criticism, until then forbidden to them. The 40 years since then have seen the Bible and its understanding restored to its central position as the primary source of Christian faith. His encyclical *Mystici Corporis* (1943) returned to the theme of the church as the body of Christ, a community that shared a common life. His *Mediator Dei* (1947) took up the theme of Jesus Christ as the one mediator between God and man. His work was brought to completion at Vatican II when the problems we have seen in structure, belief and worship were addressed and solutions proposed. We will deal with those solutions in our treatment of the work of Vatican II in Part III .

A balanced appraisal of the work of Trent must acknowledge that its careful definition of the Catholic faith reformed and renewed the church at a critical juncture in its history. Trent's doctrinal definitions gave a clarity and a comprehensiveness to the Catholic possession of the Christian message greater than that achieved in the 18 councils that preceded it. As far as the reason for being summoned — to meet the challenge of the Protestant reformation — the council was successful. Christianity split into two camps but a significant portion of Christianity remained committed to the Catholic vision of the Christian faith. The council did what it was called to do and did it well.

A balanced appraisal must also recognize that Trent fashioned a form of church that lasted for four centuries. Over that span of time, the Tridentine church came to have a note of immutability, of changelessness. From a form of church shaped to respond to a particular historical crisis, the church of Trent became *the* form of church — the only one possible.

The basic decision of the Second Vatican Council was that the Counter-Reformation church created at Trent was no longer adequate to meet the needs of contemporary Christians. A different historical situation called for a different form of church. The work of Vatican II was to produce the blueprint. Familiarity with the form of church it was drawn up to replace will help in understanding Vatican II. We turn then to consider elements of the Tridentine church.

The role of the papacy. The scandals surrounding the papacy in the 14th and 15th centuries gave birth to a movement seeking to turn teaching and ruling authority in the church over to general councils of the bishops. These councils would be summoned periodically to deal with belief and practice as they affected the church universal. The movement, known as conciliarism, sought to subject the papacy to the bishops of the church. The Council of Trent effectively put an end to this movement. The papacy summoned Trent. Papal legates presided over it. All its decrees and definitions were submitted to the pope for final confirmation. The council also entrusted to the papacy the completion of work it left unfinished. This included reforming the breviary and the mass book, and preparing the catechism to be used as the basic tool for communicating the meaning of Christian belief to the lay members of the church.

In doing so, the council gave the papacy a position of dominance it never had before. For four centuries, the teaching and ruling authority of the popes became stronger, ever more expressive of what it meant to be Catholic. One way of seeing how total papal power became is to realize that in the 1,600 years prior to Trent, 18 general councils had been summoned to deal with doctrinal and disciplinary problems. Bishops, gathered in council, made the decisions. After Trent, 300 years passed before another council was convened. In the interval, the Roman pontiff and his adminstrative assistants, the cardinals of his curia, dealt with whatever crisis the church might face.

When another council was called (Vatican I, 1870), its principal work turned out to be an endorsement of the pope's supreme teaching and ruling power in defining his infallible teaching authority. One-hundred years were to pass before another council, Vatican II, was assembled in 1962. Thus, the church created at Trent was dominated in ensuing centuries by an ever more powerful papacy. The organizational structure of the church became monarchical. As it did, the co-responsibility of the bishops for the life of the whole church, exercised so actively in the early ages of the church, disappeared in any meaningful sense.

Language for doctrine. In the early sessions of the Council of Trent, some bishops wanted to return to biblical language and theology to express Christian belief. For a time it appeared they would prevail but ultimately the council decided (under strong pressure from theologians who were trained in philosophical theology) to use the language of Thomas Aquinas and the medieval scholastics to define the meaning of Christianity. This decision had an abiding effect on the way the Christian faith was expressed in succeeding centuries. The philosophy of Thomas Aquinas became the primary, almost the sole, vehicle for presenting the Catholic belief. Gradually, the conviction grew that Christian doctrine had found in Thomistic philosphy the perfect instrument of expression. The conclusion was that not only were the truths of faith to be accepted but they were to be accepted in the way Thomism expressed them. Or, to put the matter another way, divine revelation had found in the language of Aquinas its ultimately perfect formulation. No other way of expressing the faith could add anything. Christian faith was Thomistic faith. Attempts to find other ways to speak of divine revelation, even though they might have been more comprehensible to members of the church, met immovable resistance from church authority. Faith and Thomism was the perfect marriage. To think otherwise was close to heretical.

Carrying out the council's mandate, the pope produced a catechism of the Council of Trent. It expressed Christian faith in question and answer form and became the basic source for communicating Christian faith to generations of Catholics. Brought to America, it became the *Baltimore Cathechism,* the source book of faith for untold numbers of Catholic children and adults. Catholic faith was Tridentine faith as expressed in the catechism.

Ultimately, this produced a Catholic mentality that saw Christian belief as having two inseparable aspects: the truths of revelation, and the manner of expressing those truths. Both were seen as objects of the Christian's act of faith.

The final fruit of this Tridentine legacy has been an almost pathological inability on the part of many Catholics to accept what is a contemporary truism: There is no such thing as one perfect expression of truth. People speak of what is meaningful to them in many different ways. Each age finds its own ways to possess and express the Christian faith. Trent's legacy can be a heavy burden because its only criterion for judging authentic faith is whether it is expressed in Tridentine terms. If so, it is the faith of our fathers; if not, it is heresy.

Vatican II decided that the Tridentine/Thomistic formulation of the faith was no longer apt. Pope John XXIII expressed well what became a guiding principle for the council when he said, "The substance of the ancient doctrine of the deposit of faith is one thing, and the way in which it is presented is another." At Vatican II and since the church has been exploring other ways of understanding the deposit of faith. This process is a threat to faith only for those unable to distinguish what is believed from the way it is expressed.

The nature of the church. Trent's emphasis on the position of the papacy, the role of bishops; and the status of ordained priests tended to produce a particular model for speaking of the nature of the church. Like any large, complex institution — a corporation, for example — the church was to be thought of in hierarchical terms. It could be likened to a pyramid with the pope at the summit possessing supreme teaching and ruling authority. He was, in turn, assisted in the administration of the church by his cardinal advisers. Bishops exercised absolute authority in their own dioceses. Pastors were seen as having the same position in the parishes. Finally, forming the broad base of the pyramid were the laity. Viewing the church in this way tended to divide it into active and passive members. There were the teaching and the taught, the governing and the governed. A sociological model took the place of the biblical model. The community of believers, the body of Christ, the people of God became in the Tridentine institution presided over by the clergy with the laity as subjects. Roles expressed this understanding of the church's nature. Both clergy and laity knew their place and acted accordingly. While Protestantism moved toward giving the laity an active role, Roman Catholicism reserved all active roles to the clergy.

Vatican II moved toward replacing this institutional model by returning to biblical images to speak of the church. But from Trent to Vatican II the church was, by and large, seen by both members and the world in general as made up of two groups — the clergy exercising absolute teaching and ruling authority, the laity as subjects who obeyed without questioning.

The changeless church. We have mentioned that the form of church created at Trent gradually acquired immutability. The point is important if the current struggle over change in the church is to be understood.

The manner of worshiping God, the way of expressing faith, and the hierarchical structure came to be seen, after Trent, as *the* form of church life. A form of church developed to meet the specific historical crises of the Reformation became, with the passage of time, *the* form of church. The church had reached its perfect form. There would not be — indeed, could not be — any reason for changing it. In a world characterized by waves of change as the medieval world became the modern world, one institution remained unchanged, untouched by the currents swirling all around it. The church was changeless — this was the way it always had been and always would be. In brief, the Tridentine church was an historical institution. In the midst of historical change it existed changeless, outside the flow of history. And there was a sense of security in belonging to such a church.

This picture may seem overdrawn to the point of caricature. But the measure of its accuracy is the alarm and resistance that greeted Vatican II's decision to replace the Tridentine church with a form more suited to the contemporary world. How could the church change? Had it not always been this way? Even the asking — the question revealed how completely the Counter-Reformation church had lost its sense of history, its awareness that in the 16 centuries prior to Trent, history and the church had interacted, with each shaping the other.

The church and the modern world. One final characteris-

tic of the Tridentine church calls for notice. It was perhaps
the most tragic element of Trent's legacy. It was so tragic
because it excluded the church from any significant part
in shaping the modern world. In the centuries following
Trent, the church tended to identify itself with the *ancient
regime,* with things as they once were. The mentality
adopted by the church's leadership saw the order of society
of the 16th century as a divinely ordained state of affairs:
Monarchy, kings, noble men, commoners, peasants, the
church supreme in matters of belief and practice and supported by the power of the state. This was the structure of
society as God willed it. Changing that order meant that
the forces of modernity sweeping the world in the 18th,
19th and 20th centuries found in the church an implacable
foe. Democracy, freedom of conscience, freedom of speech,
and freedom of the press met opposition and condemnation.
Because these forces shaped the modern world, it was
fashioned with little reference to the church by men who
saw the church as irrelevant, obscurantist and unalterably
opposed to progress.

Thus in the long stretch of history from the 16th to the
20th century, from Trent to Vatican II, the pattern of church
life set at Trent entrenched itself ever more firmly. Papal
dominance became increasingly stronger, reaching its
zenith in the definition of papal infallibility at the first
Vatican Council in 1870 and finding its fullest expression
in the 19th and 20th century Roman pontiffs.

The distrust, suspicion and condemnation of the modern
world grew progressively more all-embracing and produced
a Catholic life increasingly withdrawn and defensive. Finally, attempts to find ways other than those of Trent for
expressing the Christian message met with ruthless condemnation. A look at a few of the elements of this developing
pattern will help to see the ever more deeply etched linea-
ments of the image the church presented to the world. It

will also show what a dramatic about-face the council made
on the church's relationship to the world, especially in *The
Constitution on the Church in the Modern World.*

Chapter 5

The Papacy from Gregory XV (1831-46) to Pius XII (1939-58)

For western Europe, the French and American Revolutions signaled the end of monarchy as the most acceptable form of government and the beginning of a new age of democracy and individual rights. In political terms, the modern world was being born.

As the 19th century advanced, it became increasingly evident that this restructuring of society was the wave of the future. In spite of that, the church continued to look back to things as they had always been. Gregory XVI (1831-46) was the first of the 19th century popes to confront and condemn the emerging modern world, and he did it in the strongest possible terms. His 1832 encyclical *Mirari Vox* rejected popular sovereignty — the right of the people to choose their own form of government — in favor of monarchy. He strongly supported the continuation of the marriage between church and state, with the state supporting the church with its coercive power. He saw the right of individuals to form and follow their own conscience as a pernicious evil. Had it not been the responsibility of the church from time immemorial to shape people's consciences? To reject that authority would produce moral chaos. A press free to publish its own view of the meaning of human affairs was madness. How could errors expressed so frequently in the press have any right to be published? The papal voice went unheard outside the church. The forces of liberalism grew stronger. The papacy, along with the church it ruled, found itself increasingly cut off from the world.

Pius IX (1846-78) came to the papal throne in 1846 for what turned out to be the longest pontificate in history: 32 years. He added his voice to Gregory's in his famous *Syllabus of Errors* (1864). In this document Pius issued, in 80 propositions, a blanket condemnation of progress and modern civilization. The last of the propositions catches the spirit of the document rather well. It says, "The Roman pontiff can and ought not to reconcile and harmonize himself with progress, with liberalism and with modern civilization." Pius' message was clear: The world could expect no acceptance or accommodation from the church.

Pius' second major contribution to the continuing papal rejection of the modern world took the form of a general council of the church. His summoning of the First Vatican Council in 1870 and its chief work, the definition of papal infallibility, need to be seen in historical context. As the 19th century advanced, papal opposition to the new world being shaped had grown increasingly intransigent. The consequence had been an ever widening gulf between church and world. The world went its way and the church hers; the church influenced society less and less. Without the approval of the church, indeed in spite of her strong disapproval, the modern world was being born. Secular society was the victor.

The papacy recognized the situation. This awareness played a paramount part in Pius' decision to call the council. He saw need for a church victory; the rightness of the papal position must be vindicated. The announcement of the council implied it would do for the 19th century what Trent had done for the 16th. Then the enemy had been Protestantism; now it was liberalism. Trent had successfully repelled the first assault on orthodoxy. This council would achieve a similar victory over liberalism.

The council produced the result Pius desired. Eighty-eight bishops who opposed the definition of papal infallibility as inopportune left the night before the final vote. An overwhelming majority (535-2) resulted. The definition carefully spelled out the conditions for its exercise: The Roman pontiff is infallible when, as successor of Peter and head of the church universal, he speaks on matters of faith and morals and makes clear his intention to bind the conscience of all church members. The power, rarely used since its definition, produced two results, one immediate and one long-term. The immediate result was the one hoped for by the papacy and its supporters. The council was saying the popes were right in their ringing condemnation of the modern world. Their voice spoke the truth. The council's message was read in this way by the faithful and they accepted the church's rejection of the world. Catholicism retreated within the walls of its citadel of truth and rightness. The long-term result was that the definition became an umbrella gradually extended over almost every papal utterance. As the aura of infallibility extended to an ever widening field, more and more encyclicals and papal pronouncements came to be seen as infallible.

The 80 years from Leo XIII (1878-1903) to Pius XII (1939-58) produced mixed results. There were some hopeful developments. Externally, the relationship between church and world was largely characterized by continuing withdrawal and condemnation.

On the bright side, Leo realized the church should try to help solve the grave problems in the world. His encyclical *Rerum Novarum* (1891) addressed the desperate problems created for workers by the Industrial Revolution. It defended the workers' right to unionize, to strike, and to own property. Above all, the encyclical signaled an abrupt about-face in papal policy regarding society and its problems. Leo was saying the church had both a right and a duty to try to solve one of society's gravest problems. He began the move toward openness and involvement and away from withdrawal. Still, it was only a beginning. There was little implementation of Leo's vision. In theory, he initiated a reversal of the policy of withdrawal; in actuality, his document represented only a blueprint and a hope.

On the dark side, Leo continued the papal tradition of viewing the modern world with suspicion and distrust. His 1885 encyclical *Immortale Dei* reaffirmed this view. In a half-hearted way, it conceded that democracy might be an acceptable form of government: "The greater or less participation of the people in government has nothing blamable in itself." But it went on to condemn freedom of thought and freedom of the press as sources of many evils. *Longinqua Oceani,* an encyclical addressed to the American church in 1895, reflected Leo's commitment to a world that was rapidly disappearing. "It would be very erroneous," he wrote, "to draw the conclusion that in America is to be sought the hope of the most desirable status of the church, or that it would be universally lawful or expedient for state and church to be, as in America, dissevered and divorced." In other words, society in which the state supported the church was preferable to one where church and state were separate. Having said the old order was to be preferred to the new, Leo reached the obvious conclusion: Since the world is what it is, not what it should be, faithful members of the church should have little to do with that world." Unless forced by necessity to do otherwise, Catholics ought to prefer to associate with Catholics." Thus Leo's pontificate reflected both bright promise and somber actuality.

Leo was followed by Pius X (1903-1914). Pius' tenure also had its bright and dark sides. The dark side appeared in the so-called "modernist crisis." The crisis had its roots in attempts by Catholic scholars to express doctrine in ways other than that of the council of Trent. The philosophical language of Thomas Aquinas used at Trent had achieved a near monopoly in the expression of doctrine. Leo XIII had contributed to this by describing the teaching of St. Thomas as the true expression of Catholicism and by instructing seminaries to use Thomism as the basis for their philosophical and theological studies.

Toward the close of Leo's pontificate, Catholic scholars, recognizing that Thomism represented but one way to express the Christian faith, began searching for other more understandable ways. Biblical and historical studies outside the church had made great advances in the 19th century. Now Catholic scholars were beginning to use the fruits of that work in formulating the Christian message in contemporary language and thought patterns. In this way, they hoped to close the gap between the church and the modern world.

When Pius became pope, his curial advisers alerted him to the dangers of the new scholarship and urged swift and stern measures. In their view any deviation from the Tridentine formulation was not only dangerous but would destroy the content of Christian revelation. Pius took their advice. In July 1907 he issued a blanket condemnation of any attempt to present doctrine in other than Thomistic terms. The tone of the document and of the encyclical which followed it within a few months made quite clear that any new idea in theology, church history or scripture study was suspect.

Close on the heels of Pius' condemnation a full scale attack on those scholars in the church suspected of using these new ideas or of trying to deal with modern thought in a positive way was launched by the Roman curia. An army of almost a thousand informants was enlisted; their purpose was to search out and report to Rome those suspected of modernism. The witchhunt was on and it lasted until Benedict XV ended it in 1914. While it lasted, many of the church's most respected scholars felt its fury.

Benedict ended it but by then irreparable damage had been done, or, to put it the other way around, orthodoxy had been saved from the corruption of modern thought. Whichever way put, the condemnation and the campaign which followed it effectively guaranteed that Catholic biblical and historical studies would have no contact with nineteenth and twentieth century developments in these areas outside the church. Yet again the church rejected the world and turned in on itself, preferring the safety of the fortress to the dangers outside its walls.

Condemnation was not, however, the only side to Pius' reign. He had spent seventeen years as a parish priest. In consequence his own natural inclination was pastoral and that pastoral concern expressed itself in a variety of ways that strengthened the interior life of the church. He was devoted to good liturgical music and restored Gregorian chant to the liturgy. He was much concerned about the training of future priests and gave a good deal of attention to improving diocesan seminaries. He began the reform of the church's code of canon law and reformed the breviary. And he is perhaps best remembered for his 1905 decree which encouraged the daily reception of the Eucharist.

On the dark side the relation to the modern world worsened during Pius' pontificate and the legacy of distrust of modern thought he left the church was not dispelled until well into the 50's and early 60's. On the positive side much that he did renewed and strengthened the internal life of the church and held bright promise for the future.

Benedict XV (1914-22) succeeded Pius. The years of his pontificate were spent in the shadow of the first world war and its aftermath. In those years Benedict worked tirelessly for peace both inside the church and out. Inside the church he stopped the excesses of the modernist witch hunt. Peace was restored to the church but it was an uneasy peace maintained only at the price of a continued boycott of modorn thought. In consequence Roman Catholic scholarship became a synonym for sterility.

In his dealing with the Great Powers engaged in war Benedict was respected as a superb diplomat. But when he made proposals for working out a just peace they turned a deaf ear to his suggestions. A world that had been repeatedly rejected and condemned by the papacy was not about to listen to his advice. The church had chosen withdrawal from the world. The choice was respected. Peace terms werc finally agreed upon but they were arrived at without reference to the proposals of Benedict.

The pontificate of Pius XI (1922-39) initiated the final stages of papal absolutism, an absolutism that would reach its high-water mark in the reign of his successor, Pius XII. Pius XI had a strong consciousness of his supreme teaching authority and he expressed that consciousness by dealing in authoritative terms with a wide variety of subjects ranging from his encyclical on the education of the young which prohibited co-educational schools to his ringing condemnation of communism in 1937. Thus did he extend the field of his strongly authoritarian teaching well beyond the limits which had been observed by his predecessors.

Yet this absolute monarch, almost paradoxically, gave strong support and encouragement to the role of the laity in the church. The later years of his pontificate saw the emergence, particularly in American of a number of Catholic lay movements. The Christian Family movement was born; lay edited Catholic journals of opinion began to appear; care for the poor and the homeless found expression in the work of Dorothy Day and Catherine Doherty. Light and shadow were again the characteristics of the papal reign.

Pius XII (1939-58) was the apex and the end of the counter-reformation church that began at Trent and he was the final stage of the papal absolutism so characteristic of that church. Pius was a highly complex combination of deep spirituality, astute displomatic skill, personal humility and an almost obsessive awareness of his position as supreme pontiff of the Roman Catholic church. Like his predecessor he ruled with an iron hand yet his was a personality of great charm and warmth. He never spoke out against Nazism and particularly the Nazi persecution of the Jews yet his charity in providing the Jews with food, shelter and escape from Germany was boundless. He was in many ways a reactionary, identifying with the prior 19th and 20th century pontiffs in their rejection and condemnation of the world yet he was very much aware of the world situation and of modern thought and he opened the world of biblical scholarship to Catholic scholars.

The list of paradoxes in his reign could be almost indefinitely extended. Perhaps the best summary of his work is to see it as a paradox in light of what happened after him. Through much of what he did and said he laid the foundation for the work of the Second Vatican Council, yet he would have been deeply disturbed and strongly opposed to much of the reform in the church begun at the Council.

Conclusion — Part I ended with the conclusion that Christianity had lived its life in a variety of ways in the first sixteen hundred years of its existence, each way manifesting an adaptation to the circumstances of history in which that life was lived. Part II looked at the council of Trent and the form of church characterized by an unparalleled development of papal supremacy and an ever more strongly expressed condemnation of the modern world. That Tridentine church ended with the death of Pius XII. The election of John XXIII (1958-63) brought the beginning of a dramatically new era in the history of the church. We turn in Part III to a discussion of that era.

PART III:

The Renewal Church

Chapter 6

The Second Vatican Council

From the beginning of his pontificate John made clear his vision of the church called for significant changes in its life. He called it *aggiornamento* updating; a general council was his instrument. As the council began in 1962, he spelled out what he hoped from it. He disassociated himself from those in the church who "in these modern times can see nothing but prevarication and ruin," who say "that our era, in comparison with past eras, is getting worse." Instead, he was hopeful, and he urged the council to be. "Divine Providence," he said, "is leading us to a new order of human relations." To follow that lead the council must "look to the present, to the new conditions and new forms of life introduced into the modern world." The council's responsibility was to shape a church able to serve the needs of this new world and to spread "everywhere the fullness of Christian charity."

The majority of the council adopted John's vision of hope. Out of its deliberations over four years (1962-65) emerged the blueprint for a church intended to replace the church of Trent. The council documents signaled the end of the withdrawn, defensive, condemnatory, Counter-Reformation church and the beginning of a servant church that existed not to condemn but to serve the world.

The first council documents to be promulgated was the *Constitution on the Liturgy*. By its first pronouncement, the council was saying the spirit of the renewed church would be most aptly expressed and most surely communicated to the members in its worship. Put back into the language of the people, the reformed liturgy was to involve the full and active participation of all the faithful. All were to realize that the liturgy was a call to and an expression of union with one another. All eat the same bread of life and all come to share the same life. The result is to be community, and strong emphasis was put on developing it. The eucharistic liturgy's primary purpose was to prepare those who came together around the table of the Lord for service to each other and to the world. Community and preparation for service, the document was saying, are at the heart of liturgical worship.

This first document set the direction for the rest of the council. The manner of worshiping God characteristic of the church of Trent — the priest saying mass in an unintelligible language with the faithful as passive spectators occupied with their private prayers and devotions — was to be replaced by a eucharistic liturgy understood and participated in by all. Private devotion was to yield to communal worship. Notice was being served that the council intended to create a new form of church with liturgy as a primary expression of its meaning.

Next came the *Constitution on the Church*. This document is noteworthy for its answer to three very sensitive questions: How is the nature of the church best described? What is the relationship between the bishops and the pope? What is the role of Mary in the church?

The Tridentine model of church was sociological. The church is a society with a set of beliefs and rules that the membership accepts as binding. It is a structured organization with power to teach, to sanctify and to govern. That power is possessed in its fullness by the Roman pontiff and, in subordination to him, by the bishops and priests. The subjects of this power are the lay members. Church language was juridical. It spoke of rights and responsibilities, of powers and duties, of rulers and subjects.

At Vatican II, the bishops decided such language was inappropriate and inadequate. For their description of the church, they turned to the imagery of scripture. The church is an organism, not an organization. She is the body of Christ called to make him continually present in the world. The church is a community, not a society. She is a fellowship of believers bound together by sharing the same life. Ruler and subject are inappropriate for describing the relationship between members. All enter the community by the same door, Baptism; hence all are equally members of the community. All are committed to serve the needs of the community and of the world; members are distinguished only in their form of service. Some serve by teaching and leading the people of God; others serve by the witness of their caring lives. And there is one in the community whose proudest title should be "the servant of the servants of God."

The document on the church does not read like a theological textbook with philosophical or sociological language describing an objective, identifiable structure; instead, vivid scriptural images speak of a pilgrim people, a servant community, a fellowship of believers, and, ultimately, of a mystery, not an organization.

In its second major emphasis, *The Constitution on the Church* took up a question left unanswered at the First Vatican Council. It intended to deal with governance in the church. *Schemata* were prepared on the roles of the pope and the bishops. However, the political situation in Italy was such that the council was able to deal only with the ruling and teaching power of the Roman pontiff. It never got to the complementary role of the bishops. This failure played no small part in the subsequent expansion of the papal role in the church.

Vatican II took up this unfinished business. Regarding the role of the bishops, the council spelled out the notion of collegiality. It holds that the bishops as successors of the apostles share with the successor of Peter responsibility not just for their dioceses but for the church universal. The council's document was delicately suggesting the church was constitutional rather than monarchical. Further, it suggested the pope should rely on the bishops and act in conjunction with them in exercising his teaching and ruling authority. This would incorporate into church governance a worldwide vision of the gospel message's meaning. In other words, the document was hinting that the time had come in the Roman Catholic church for emphasizing *Catholic* instead of *Roman*.

The council dealt with another problem left unresolved at Trent. Addressing the issue of the church's organizational structure, it suggested that the teaching and ruling role the bishops had exercised in the early church might be restored. This thinking came, in part, from the fact that the bishops had come from the four corners of the earth. As such a diverse group, they saw there was more than one answer to the question, "What does it mean to be Christian in today's world?" In fact, there were a variety of answers shaped by the different needs of people in various parts of the world.

The third sensitive area addressed by the document was Mary and her role in the church. Through the 19th and 20th centuries, devotion to Mary had assumed an ever more prominent place in the devotional life of the church. One need only mention Fatima, Lourdes and Pius XII's definition of the doctrine of the assumption. In line with this trend, a significant segment of bishops felt that an entire document should be devoted to describing Mary's privileges and the particular place she occupied in Catholic life. On the other hand, some bishops felt treating Mary in a separate document would imply she was not a member of the church but was above it and stood as mediator between the church and her son. They believed this would distort the scriptural picture of Mary. The Bible, they said, clearly speaks of Mary as a member of the first Christian community that received the outpouring of the Spirit on Pentecost. They did not want to treat Mary apart from the church. They wanted to speak of her role in the document on the church. When the vote came, they prevailed. In line with this decision, a chapter of Mary was added to the document on the church. No special document on Mary was issued by the council.

The bishops drew their image of Mary from the scripture and the fathers of the church rather than the sometimes exaggerated language of the devotions that had developed in recent centuries. They were careful to situate Mary in the church. Scripture describes her as always close to her son and as the exemplar of what it means to be his disciple. She is the first Christian, the preeminent member of the community of her son's followers; she is a member of the church, not above it.

The council's next major document was the *Constitution on Divine Revelation*. It and the *Constitution on the Church* are the council's two most fundamental documents. Christianity is faith in God's revelation to mankind. People come to faith in the church and through her teaching of revelation. Thus revelation and church are basic to Christian belief. As with the church, the understanding of revelation underwent major revision at the council. The document on revelation should be read as another expression of the council's avowed purpose of replacing the Counter-Reformation church with one more attuned to the contemporary world. In this connection, three major emphases emerge.

The first occurs in the initial chapters of the document where the nature of revelation and the way it is transmitted are discussed. When confronted with the Protestant assertion that scripture alone is the source of saving knowledge, Trent had responded with its "two-source" theory of revelation. God gives his revelation to mankind through scripture and through tradition, the constant teaching of the church. This two-source theory produced four centuries of bitter controversy.

At Vatican II, the bishops took a new approach. God is the single source of revelation. That revelation is communicated through scripture and through tradition. But they were not distinguished in the document as distinct "sources" of revelation. "Sacred tradition and scripture are like a mirror in which the pilgrim church on earth looks at God" (Article 7). "Hence there exists a close connection and communication between sacred tradition and sacred scripture. For both of them, flowing from the same divine well spring, in a certain way, merge into a unity and tend toward the same end" (Article 9).

The shift may seem subtle. Nevertheless, it represents a break with the two-source theory of Trent and presents the Catholic understanding of revelation in terms more acceptable to Protestantism. In a definite movement away from the Counter-Reformation church, the council was saying: We want to find a way of understanding revelation more congenial to our separated brethren.

Chapters 2-5 of the constitution contained the second major emphasis. Again, there is a significant shift away from the mindset of the Tridentine church. At the beginning of this century, resistance to the modern world resulted in a sweeping condemnation of Catholic scholars who sought to deal with contemporary thought in positive terms. The aftermath of this condemnation had been a half-century of repressing many of the best minds in the church. The first break in the resistance to modern scholarship had come with Pius XII's 1943 encyclical *Divino Afflante Spiritu*. In it, he instructed Catholic biblical scholars to begin using the historical and critical methods for studying the scripture that Protestants had been developing for a century. The council's document on revelation, issued 20 years after Pius had opened Catholic scholarship to modern thought, represented some of the fruits of the work done during that period.

In speaking of the interpretation of scripture, the document adopted some of the basic guidelines used by contemporary biblical scholarship. To understand scripture, one must make every effort to get at the meaning intended by the author. To do this it is necessary to get back into the world of the sacred writer and discover the ways used at that time to speak of religious belief. In other words, one must set aside a 20th-century mindset and think as a first-century believer in Jesus if one is to grasp the meaning of the gospels. Doing that means paying attention to literary forms, searching out the historical circumstances, and trying to discover the kind of community for which the evangelist wrote his gospel. Having done all that, one is able to understand what the author intended, not just what the text says.

Using this mode of interpretation, the document speaks of the meaning of both the Old and New Testament. In so doing, it lays to rest the church's resistance to modern biblical thought. Further, it makes clear that Vatican II will use contemporary thought to make the Christian message accessible to today's world.

The final chapter treats scripture in the life of the church. It deals decisively with Trent's refusal to address the question of vernacular versions of the Bible and the consequent inaccessibility of the word of God to the faithful. "Easy access to the sacred scripture should be provided for all the

Christian faithful" (Article 22). Vernacular versions of the Bible are mandated. Scripture is to become the central theme of all preaching in the church. "All the preaching of the church must be nourished and ruled by sacred scripture." (Article 21) The use of th best contemporary methods for studying scripture is also strongly endorsed. "This sacred synod encourages the sons of the church who are biblical scholars to continue energetically with the work they have so well begun" (Article 23). Lastly, all members of the church are urged to read and study the scripture and to form their spirituality in its message.

Thus did the fathers of the council restore the word of God to its central position as the chief source of Christian truth and the fountainhead of authentic Christian spirituality.

Two other documents issued by the council underscored the determination of the majority of the bishops to break the church out of its Tridentine mold. When the council was convened, four centuries had elapsed since the Protestant reformers had separated from Roman Catholicism in order to develop a Christian church that they felt more faithfully reflected the Christianity expressed in the Bible. The intervening centuries had been marked by bitterness, by mutual distrust and hatred, and even by bloodshed. To each side, the Christianity of the other was a corrupt, deformed expression of the Christian message. Faced with this situation, the bishops decided the time had come for the Roman church to acknowledge the continuing scandal of a fragmented Christianity and to take decisive action toward finding a solution to the separation.

The Decree on Ecumenism was the result of that decision. It was a remarkable document, representing a complete about-face in the Roman church's attitude toward the reunion of the Christian churches. For Rome, reunion has always meant the return of the separated churches to the mother church they had left.

Adopting a different point of view, this document begins with the church acknowledging her share of guilt for the hatred, bloodshed and scandal that marked the centuries of separation. The divisions among Christian churches result from sin on both sides. For the Roman Catholic church's sins against unity the bishops say, "in humble prayer, we beg pardon of God and of our separated brethren, just as we forgive those who trespass against us" (Article 7).

From the admission of guilt, the decree moves on to insist that reunion must be the concern of all Catholics. Elements of a call to action are spelled out: continuing prayer for reunion, a renewed commitment to the Catholic tradition, a conscientious effort to understand the faith commitment of the separated brethren, a willingness to dialogue objectively and with charity and, finally, an involvement with all Christians in bringing Christianity to bear on the social problems of today's world.

The document is realistic in acknowledging much still divides the churches but makes clear reunion does not simply mean return. Both parties must accept responsibility for reunion and work toward it. However, healing the divisions among the churches will not be brought about by human effort. All the Christian churches need to acknowledge that the unity is the clear will of the Lord, whom all serve. Acknowledging that should produce a concerted effort by all to heal the wounds and bring about reunion. Having done all they can, Christians must turn their efforts over to the Spirit of unity. He will in his time and in his way transform this human effort into a solution to the problem that Christians cannot solve themselves.

The council's final major document was issued the day before it closed, December 8, 1965. This document, the *Con-*

stitution on the Church in the Modern World, brought together all that the council tried to accomplish. The title suggests its content: church and world.

Further, the title points to the relationship that should exist between church and world. The church is to be *in* the world, not apart from it. The constitution offers a sweeping and perceptive analysis of the contemporary world and its problems. It touches the dignity of the human person and the community of mankind. It deals with marriage and family, contemporary culture, mankind's economic and social life, the political community, and peace and brotherhood among nations.

The tone throughout is positive. The appraisal of cultural expressions and social and economic trends is realistic and sympathetic. The wholesale rejections of the past are missing; instead, there is a sincere attempt to understand the world, to endorse much of what it stands for, and to outline what service the church might offer as it works toward peace and justice.

The analysis ends with a moving call to the church's membership and to the whole human family:

"The proposals of this sacred synod look to the assistance of every man of our time, whether he believes in God, or does not explicitly recognize him. Their purpose is to help men gain a sharper insight into their full destiny, so that they can fashion the world more to man's surpassing dignity, search for a brotherhood which is universal and more deeply rooted, and meet the urgencies of our age with a gallant and unified effort born of love" (Article 91).

Thus in its final document the council expressed in forceful and concrete language its avowed purpose of leading the church out of the fortress built at Trent. The council's mandate and challenge to church members was clear:

Begin again to celebrate in your worship that you are a community of service; take up again the word of God as it is spoken in scripture and nourish your interior life on its message; set aside your fear and your distrust of Christians who do not fully share your faith; learn to understand, to love, to collaborate with them. Above all, let this renewed commitment to your Christian heritage lead you into the world. Be there; be concerned; be involved. Carry your faith into the marketplace of the world and cooperate with all people of good will in an effort to produce a world of charity, of justice and of peace.

Chapter 7

Since Vatican II

During the Second Vatican Council well over 2,000 bishops from every part of the world met in Rome for four years and produced 16 documents. These documents, confirmed and promulgated by Paul VI, represented a consensus of Roman Catholic leadership. They spelled out a form of church that the bishops intended as a replacement for the church of Trent.

We are now 20 years distance from the council. How has its blueprint fared? I believe one can begin to answer by saying that the single most significant result of the council has been to open the question of what it means to be a Catholic.

The question receives two basic answers in today's church. One comes from those who prefer the church as it was. In broad strokes, they prefer a Christianity that is private and individual. One leads a good life, obeys the commandments, goes to church and receives the sacraments, and hopes, at death, to be in the state of grace and worthy of being received into God's presence for eternity. They accept the mass in English (though some prefer Latin) but not its implications of community and service. They are comfortable with faith as expressed in the language of Trent and the catechism they learned as children. They are uneasy with biblical scholarship, preferring a literal interpretation of the Bible's meaning.

The organizational structure of the Counter-Reformation church is for them the way the church ought to be, has always been. This means a strong papacy and a commitment to the papal position as the only possible position for Catholics. They willingly accept clerical leadership and domination. They do not want to be given a sense of the history of the church because it can pose serious problems for their faith. Ecumenism means for them what it has always meant: return of Protestants to the one true church. Separation and wariness continue to be their attitudes toward Protestantism.

Devotion to Mary still occupies a very special place in their lives. They are confused and scandalized by what they see to be a de-emphasis on Marian devotion in today's church. Finally, they find the new approach to morality with its emphasis on love rather than law not only unacceptable but clearly dangerous.

A considerable number in this group are clergy who find their traditional role in the church seriously threatened by the church of Vatican II. Since they are in positions of leadership and authority, and since that position is accepted by a substantial percentage of the laity, they are able to block implementation of Vatican II's mandates and retain things as they are.

The second group wants the church of Vatican II implemented. Leaders of this group include the clergy who have made a sincere attempt to become aware of the council's directives. They have instituted liturgical reform in their parishes and are trying to build community. They recognize the social implications of Christianity and their homilies stress Christian responsibility for the world's needs. They have implemented the notion of collegiality, or shared responsibility, setting up parish councils and involving parishioners in determining what shape the life of their parish should take.

Many religious congregations of women are in this group. Their lives of withdrawal have yielded to lives of involvement in the needs of the church and the world. Continual reading and study keep them abreast of developments within the church. Their understanding of the meaning of the Christian life and their living of it constitutes a bright hope for the future of the church.

Included, too, are the laity who are open to the vision of the council. They read, attend seminars, meet in groups to study and pray. They want to develop a sense of their history, hoping it will help them to shape a contemporary and meaningful faith. They are eager for an understanding of the word of God, realizing that it is the wellspring of their faith. Because life presents continuously serious moral dilemmas, they look for help from the best of today's moral theology. They recognize the social implications of their faith and are informed about and involved in the great issues of our times: war and peace, justice, discrimination, nuclear arms. They expect the clergy to accept them as equal members of the church. They want to work with the clergy in creating community and sharing responsibility for the life of the parish.

The stance of the first group since the council has been one of resisting implementation of the council's mandates. Members of this group have done so for what they see as the most compelling of reasons: the preservation of the church as it should be. A discussion of recent developments within the church follows. As we proceed, remember that a substantial segment of the church's membership opposes these developments. Moreover, this group may well prevail in its struggle to restore the church to what it was before the council.

Social Christianity. Perhaps the strongest development

since the council has been an increase in the awareness of
the responsibility for the church to be in the world, concerned about the world's problems, and involved in working
for their solutions. The result has been a shift in the way
many members of the church understand and live their
faith. In the pre-conciliar church Christian living was an
essentially private affair. One obeyed the commandments,
avoided sin and frequented mass and the sacraments. The
virtue of charity was very much part of a Christian's life
but its expression focused on caring for the needs of family
and neighbors, on supporting the church's missionary activity by prayer and financial contribution, and on giving bas-
kets for the poor at Thanksgiving and Christmas. Larger
issues such as peace among nations, freedom and justice
for all people, world poverty and hunger, nuclear armament
and discrimination were rarely seen as the individual
Christian's responsibility.

Since the council, a growing number of Christians have
come to see that Christian living has an essentially social
dimension. Charity is at the heart of the Christian vocation.
Anyone in need, next door or across the world, has a claim
on the concern of the Christian. Problems plaguing the
world — whether the threat of war, discrimination, oppres-
sion — are a Christian responsibility.

Two developments in particular have contributed to this
new sense of global responsibility. The first is the renewed
liturgical life of the church. At its best, liturgy produces
two results. First, sharing the bread of life with fellow
Christians in the celebration of the eucharist brings with
it a growing realization that Christianity is not a religion
of individuals; it is a community of believers. The bond of
shared life inevitably expresses itself in charity, in care
and concern and love for those whose lives are bound to
one's own by a common belief and a common life. Second,
the same shared liturgical life brings one to see that

eucharist is also preparation for service because it brings the life of the risen Lord. One is empowered with the same life that Christ now lives with the Father. One possesses God's own life and God is, in St. John's word, love. Eucharist makes charity the law of one's life.

Involvement in the world and its problems flows out of this realization: Eucharist mandates service. This involvement has taken a multitude of forms: opposing nuclear armament, advocating pacifism, serving the poor, working for the rights of the migrant workers, supporting freedom and justice in Central America, opposing racial or sexual discrimination. Whatever form the involvement takes, the conviction that Christianity means service is the driving force behind it.

This involvement has spread through all levels of the church. The popes speak out against the vicious cycle of poverty and the awful threat of nuclear war. Bishops become pacifists or urge their people not to work in plants where nuclear warheads are assembled. Religious women give their lives for justice in El Salvador. Parishioners set up food kitchens for the hungry and employment offices for the jobless. Priest preach social responsibility from their pulpits and join demonstrators against racial discrimination.

Yet, most Catholics are not involved in such activities. Far from it. Many oppose seeing Christianity as essentially social. For them, social activism is a source of scandal. "The church should stay out of politics." "The priest's place is the altar and the pulpit." These are complaints commonly heard. For those who think this way, and they may well be the majority, Christianity remains what it was before the council — a private, personal relationship between the individual and his or her God.

But there is a movement in the church which may yet

bring Catholics to realize that Christianity is communal
not private. We do not go to God alone; we are on pilgrimage
toward him together. A Christian's purpose is not saving
one's immortal soul. It is far more than that. It is bringing
God's world to be what he intended in creating. Liturgy
can, and in many places does, make a contribution toward
bringing people to realize this and act accordingly.

The other development contributing to the emergence of
social Christianity comes out of contemporary biblical
studies. Work on the New Testament, in particular on the
meaning and message of Jesus, has shown the core of Jesus'
preaching was that the kingdom or reign of God had arrived.
Jesus saw his own work as making the saving activity of
God present and active among human beings. God cares
for the needs of his people. This was the lesson he taught
as he cured the sick, fed the hungry, gave sight to the blind.
He saw his life's task as service: "The Son of Man has come
not to be served but to serve and to give his life in ransom
for the many."

Christ's call to those who chose to follow him was to
continue this work of service. They were to make God's
reign present after he had gone. The early Christian communities understood this mandate of love and service. The
accounts of their lives that have come down to us make
clear that commmunity and charity were hallmarks.

Over the centuries and under the pressure of historical
developments, the central message of Jesus was transformed. The kingdom of God shifted away from being an
activity — God present and caring for the needs of his
people in Jesus and then in his followers. The kingdom of
God became a place — the kingdom of heaven. The Christian did not enter the kingdom in this world by identifying
with God's care for his people. Instead, one entered after
death. Heaven became the prize to be won by those who
led good lives here on earth. For the majority, Christianity

became an individual and personal relationship with God. It remained so for many centuries.

Yet, the full meaning of being a Christian did not disappear entirely. Over the centuries, some Christians still felt the call to ministry and service. They entered the priesthood, became religious women or took up the monastic life. The Christian vocation became the province of a relatively small group in the church. What was once seen as the call of all who numbered themselves among Jesus' followers became the call of the few, considered the more generous. Christianity for the laity meant leading a good life and obeying the commandments of God and the church.

Now, under the influence of the renewed liturgy and the recovery of the central message of Jesus, the realization is growing that the Christian vocation is a universal call. It summons all Christians to enter the kingdom here on earth. In answering the summons, they enter the kingdom by accepting responsibility for the world and its people.

Morality. Closely allied with the emergence of social Christianity is a significant shift in the understanding of Christian morality. The Second Vatican Council said that "moral teaching should be more thoroughly nourished by scriptural teaching." Accepting that mandate, moral theologians have been returning to the pages of the New Testament to discover the meaning of the Christian life. Jesus, the central figure of those pages, called his followers to discipleship, to be as he was. To be as Christian, then, means to know and to follow Jesus' way of life.

The central characteristic of his life-style was concern for others whose needs he met, and for his Father, whose will he did. He fed the hungry, cured the sick, counseled and forgave the sinner. His life was other-directed. Its meaning can be summed up in the single word — love. In calling others to discipleship, he was saying that being his follower meant loving God and loving one's neighbor.

The realization that Christians are called to be as he was provides a basic premise of contemporary moral teaching. The emphasis in Christian living is not so much on avoiding what is wrong nor on obeying the commandments. Instead, the accent is on loving a person, Jesus, who is like us in all things, who is indeed what it means to be human, and on loving God and neighbor as he did. Christians are called to be human and there is one way of achieving it — following the law of love.

Christian living in light of the New Testament requires a choice. Moral theologians call it a "fundamental option." Christians are challenged to decide what sort of person they want to be. The choice is between accepting Jesus' invitation to be as he was or refusing it and choosing self and selfishness. Life is lived in light of this basic choice.

As a result, morality begins with a basic personal orientation — the choice of a way of living. Life becomes the struggle to extend love, our fundamental choice. The challenge is to extend it ever more widely, allowing it to pervade all of our actions, while, at the same time, more firmly rooting it in adherence to Jesus and his way of being human.

This perspective on morality helps to clarify the difference between the old and new ways of answering the question, what is sin? The past all too often concentrated on the act itself — theft, murder, graft, marital infidelity, dishonesty. It did not pay much attention to the act as an expression or denial of love of God and neighbor. The general inclination was to identify a good life with doing certain things and avoiding others. Morality was situated in the act rather than in the person.

Now this question is asked when a moral choice is to be made: How does the Christian express love of God and neighbor in this situation? The purpose of acting in a particular way is not primarily to make oneself better, to avoid hell or grow in grace. Instead, it is to make present and active the commitment to love as Jesus loved. Morality is the expression of the kind of person the follower of Jesus is.

A second, equally important emphasis in contemporary moral thinking is the primacy of the individual conscience in moral decision-making. Catholics have always accorded their church a major role in the formation of conscience. They do so because they believe the Holy Spirit guides and illumines the church in her teaching. The church has been a source of moral values. In practice, Catholics often looked to their church to tell them what to do, what not to do, what was sinful, what was not.

Within the past several decades, a number of developments have led many serious-minded Catholics to recognize that this attitude needs re-evaluation. Two recent examples will shape why.

1) Prior to and during World War II the German Catholic bishops decided for what they considered prudential reasons not to condemn and oppose Hitler and the Nazi regime. Not told what position they were to take on Nazism, they did little to resist Hitler. With the outbreak of the war, they found themselves tolerating, if not supporting, one of the gravest evils of this century.

2) During the first session of Vatican II, the subject of contraception was introduced on the council floor. Pope Paul VI immediately removed the issue from discussion and appointed a commission of about 65 persons, one-third priests, two-thirds laity, to study the question of birth regulation and responsible parenthood. After two years of study, the commission produced a report saying a large majority accepted the use of artificial means of contraception as morally licit. Pope Paul chose to disregard the majority opinion

and soon afterward issued his encyclical *Humanae Vitae,* which reaffirmed papal opposition to artificial contraception.

Such cases have led Catholics to ask: How can I let another, even the church, make my moral decisions? Increasingly, the answer has been the realization that the conscience of the individual Christian is and must be the immediate judge of moral action.

In light of this, how does moral theology see the adult Christian arriving at moral decisions? How do prudent men and women choose to act? Faced with possible choices, they do the following: Find out what the experts say is the right way to proceed, look to the church and its guidance, and consult the views of reputable moral theologians. They must consider the consequences of their choices. When all this has been done, they choose a course of action.

Placing the ultimate responsibility for moral choices on the individual conscience is both valuable and dangerous. Its value is that it can mean maturity in the Christian life. The danger is that it can lead to a completely subjective conscience.

One last element of contemporary moral theology calls for attention. It is the change that has occurred in thinking about the natural law. A key notion in today's moral thinking is that one is in constant interaction with one's historical situation and culture. History and culture influence the decisions that the Christian must make. The person's understanding of right and wrong is significantly and constantly affected by culture and history. Natural law is not a static thing; it is dynamic and evolving. One has a responsibility to determine how it is to be interpreted in any given age.

As the world grows more complex, people realize that simple solutions are no longer adequate. An increasing number of Christians no longer view war as a justifiable way of settling international disputes; they see that war waged with nuclear weaponry could threaten the extinction of the human race. This reading of the present historical situation has resulted in an increased interest in absolute pacifism, a stance expressed in such actions as conscientious objection, demands for a nuclear arms freeze, and refusal to pay taxes for escalating military expenditures. Moral dilemmas also present themselves in the rate at which world population is growing, the grave problems of space, repression of human rights, and world hunger and poverty. For concerned Christians, questions arise. How does a responsible Christian respond? What would Jesus ask of his followers? The contemporary approach to morality shifts the focus to the individual conscience and away from objective law. It insists that love, not law, is the supreme Christian value. It sees the natural law as a dynamic challenge, not an unchanging absolute. But not all Catholics acclaim this approach. For many, it destroys traditional moral values. They see it opening the whole area of morality to private interpretation. Accustomed to a clear set of patterns for behavior, they find this approach is too painful and confusing. For these Christians the post-Trent emphasis on changelessness creates problems. Because they are unaware of historical change and development, they can respond only with a predictable resistance to current trends in moral thinking. Lack of a sense of history leaves them ill-prepared to cope with contemporary developments in moral theology.

Understanding scripture. The dramatic developments in understanding the scriptures have made a major contribution to the life of the post-conciliar church. Following the mandate of Pius XII, Catholic biblical scholars began in the late 1940's to use the methods of biblical scholarship which Protestantism had been developing for well over a hundred years. In the decades since, use of these methods has produced a quantum leap in biblical understanding.

The basic insight in this contemporary approach has been that various parts of the Bible were written by men of cultures much different from ours. These cultures are separated from our century by anywhere from 2,000 to 4,000 years. The result is an enormous gap between the authors of the Bible and their original readers and 20th century readers.

Once this is recognized, it is only a short step to realizing that 20th century readers bring their own particular cultural and historical mindset to the reading of the Bible. They assume the text means what they understand it to mean. In other words, they assume that the question to be asked of any book of the Bible is: What does the text say? Accordingly, once that meaning is grasped, in 20th century terms, the message of the text is readily understood.

But contemporary scholarship has come to see that the appropriate question is a different one. The proper question is: What did the author of the text intend for the original audience? Answering that requires, immersing oneself in the world that produced the biblical writers and their audience. It calls for skill in biblical languages and an awareness of the history of the ancient Middle East and its peoples. One must also know the ways in which people of those times spoke and wrote of religious belief. What did they understand history to be when they made claim to writing it? For example, one needs to know the community for which John wrote his gospel — its history, its membership, its problems and its way of understanding Jesus — if one is to penetrate the meaning of his gospel.

The work of biblical criticism includes all these areas and more. It is a continuing task: the discoveries of archaeology, the meaning of ancient languages, and recognition of the

Bible as the product of a long period of oral tradition. This approach has produced an understanding of scripture quite different from that when the question was simply, what does the text say?

This development in understanding the scriptures is perhaps the most profound change to occur in the contemporary church. The revision of the liturgy is a possible exception. However, much biblical scholarship has yet to have an impact on ordinary members of the church. There are several reasons. First, much of the work is in books written by scholars for scholars; hence, it remains inaccessible to the church's membership. True, many scholars have tried to communicate the results of their work in books aimed at ordinary Christians but most people do not read them. Second, most Catholics look to priests for instruction about their faith. The most common place for this is the Sunday homily. But it is extraordinarily difficult to pass on this kind of knowledge in a brief talk. In addition, many priests are unaware of these recent developments in scripture, or, if aware, they are uncomfortable in discussing them. The situation calls for continuing programs of study.

Two other difficulties compound the problem. The first is the notion of the changelessness so characteristic of the pre-Vatican II church. When applied to scripture, this attitude holds that the meaning of the Bible is unchanging. How can one say that the meaning of the Bible differs from what has always been taught? The other, perhaps even more formidable, difficulty is that religious belief is for many people the bedrock of certainty. They perceive this new approach to understanding scripture as a threat to faith. It questions all certitude. The problems might be understood this way: Picture the reaction when the believer is told that much of the material in the infancy stories in Matthew's gospel or Luke's gospel is not historical but reflects the author's intention to make a series of theological statements. His purpose in these stories is not so much to recount history as to make a statement of belief. The reaction is predictable disillusionment. Most people's basis of faith will be shaken. This example sharply focuses the difficulty in communicating contemporary biblical scholarship. The answer lies beyond the scope of a Sunday homily. The situation also points to a need for growth in understanding the complexities and responsibilities of Christian life.

Liturgy. Implementing the directives and spirit of Vatican II is perhaps nowhere more evident than in liturgy. This does not mean that liturgical renewal has achieved perfection or been embraced with enthusiasm by all. However, the difference between celebrating the liturgy in 1960 and 1966 or 1967 is extraordinary, especially in the light of the past four centuries. Language, rubrics, vestments, accoutrements, location of the altar, and the position of the celebrant are visible evidence of renewal. Gone is the Latin mass, with the laity saying the rosary, reading a prayerbook, or communing silently with God in private prayer. In praying and singing together, in exchanging the sign of peace, in receiving the eucharist from each other, worshipers are saying: We are a community and we go to God as a people, not as individuals. Liturgy is fostering community.

The renewed liturgy has increased the realization that in receiving the body of the Lord, Christians come to possess his life. In coming together to eat the same food, the Christian community shares the same life. This bond makes a profound difference. Individual Christians are not now on their own private way to God but are traveling in community with other human beings. The eucharist is a call to service. As one possessing God's own life, the Christian is called to care. This is the bond that unites. The liturgy has been most successful in bringing individual Christians to a sense of community. There is a sense in which the liturgy now belongs to the people as well as to the clergy. The people have become active participants in liturgical ministry as lectors, ministers of the eucharist, deacons and planners of liturgy.

In liturgy, one can most surely distinguish between a parish that has accepted the council's mandate for reform and one that has not. A silent community, with each person absorbed in private prayer and unaware of other people, is a commentary on the faith of that parish. It says the Christian is an individual who believes that faith calls for a private relationship to God. It says the Christian comes to pray for individual needs, not those of the community. It says the community prefers leaving things as they are. Community singing and handshaking at the sign of peace interferes with private prayer. On the other hand, a vocal, singing, celebrating congregation says: We come here to be with each other, to eat the bread of life together, to celebrate as a community of God's care for us. We are a family and we express that in our worship.

In addition to creating a sense of community, the council expressed the hope that a renewed liturgy would foster a realization that Christians are called to service. Eating together is sharing life — in this case, the life of Jesus. The Christian possessing this life is called and empowered to be as Jesus was: to care, to heal, to console and to forgive. If Christians in eating together share the same life in Jesus, then they bear responsibility for each other and for people throughout the world. In many parishes, people reflect this both in liturgy and in day-to-day living. This was an aim of the council and is one of its biggest achievements.

Parishes committed to community develop many ways of fostering a feeling of belonging together. They have coffee after mass so that they can get to know each other; on occasions, lay members are asked to give the homily and share with the community what their faith means to them.

They develop home liturgies to give small groups the intimate experience of celebrating the eucharist with one's family, friends and neighbors. Opportunities abound within the parish and the community for service. Responding, the Christian heeds the call to ministry. The results are better liturgies, youth programs, adult education, and help for the sick, the troubled, the sorrowing and the aged. Through these ministries, those united in the bread of life serve in the manner that Jesus served.

How has the council's blueprint fared? In liturgical renewal, the answer is threefold:

1) In some parishes, little if any reform has taken place. The altar turned around and the mass in English are the sum of the renewal.

2) In many parishes, the pastor, with support of the people, has pushed liturgical renewal. These parishes have a growing sense of community and involvement.

3) The notion that eucharist calls us to service is not yet generally accepted by Catholics. Most still look on Catholicism in a private sense — living a good life. They do not see that their faith calls them to serve the needs of others.

Collegiality. Because of the church structure established after Trent, Catholics have seen authority exercised by those in power with little or no input from other members. Vatican I, after defining papal infallibility, never got around to dealing with the role of bishops. As a result, the subject came up early on Vatican II's agenda. Its key concept on episcopal authority was collegiality, or shared responsibility. This was an effort to implement a form of decision-making different from that exercised in the church in recent centuries.

An ancient belief of the church held that the bishop had the primary responsibility for his diocese. Secondly, as a direct descendant of the apostles, the bishop shared with his other bishops responsibility for the entire church. Upon definition by Vatican II, Pope Paul VI began to set up an organization allowing all the bishops to come together and participate in making decisions for the entire church. They would do this in conjunction with the pope. Paul was moving away from decision-making by one person and toward exercise of authority by a group. This was collegiality. The hope was that, because of input from the bishops, decision-making would be better informed as well as more widely shared.

Likewise, the council intended that the prinicple of collegiality should spread throughout the church. On the international level was the synod of bishops, the structure set up to bring the bishops to Rome and make decisions with the pope for the whole church. Through episcopal conferences, collegiality was exercised at the national level. Within their dioceses, bishops would not exercise authority alone. Instead, they would call together the priests who would share in making the decisions. This would continue to the next level, the parish. The pastor would call upon his associate clergy and his people to formulate the ways Christian life would be lived at the local level and what needs would be served.

The more one moves toward accepting shared responsibility, the farther one is from being told what to do. There is still the exercise of authority, but the context is different: All share in the decision-making. This puts an enormous burden on each Christian. Leadership no longer makes decisions in a pyramid structure but within a living organism in which everyone is committed to service. Christians can no longer say, as they have, that they have no opportunity to contribute service to the church. Collegiality provides a chance for all.

Assessment of collegiality is difficult at this time. Structures that exercised autonomous decision-making for centuries will not change rapidly. Some outstanding examples of collegiality have occurred. For example, Cardinal Joseph Ritter of St. Louis established a diocesanwide council. All levels and walks of life were represented. On the whole, however, the acceptance of collegiality has been slow. To the extent that some parishes have shared responsibility, the spirit and understanding of Vatican II's collegiality has taken hold.

Collegiality places tremendous responsibility on those involved. It gives lay people a new role. To be successful collegiality requires, indeed demands, people who are committed to the community, who are informed, and who view authority as service. It also requires seeing the decision-making of the Tridentine church as *a* form of exercising authority, not *the* form.

Collegiality is one of the most sensitive issues of Vatican II. Its adaptation would incorporate the meaning of the gospel message into the governance of the church. It is far too early to know whether the college of bishops will exercise the same authority over belief and practice as the college of cardinals and the curia have. It is also too early to evaluate the willingness of the laity to accept shared decision-making and the burden of responsibility resulting from the gospel's call to service.

Ecumenism. Vatican II recognized that the Christian community should be one. Unity is the Lord's will. The separation of Christian churches is a scandal. As long as they remain apart, the church is not the church of the Lord. At the Last Supper, Jesus said: "I pray, Father, that they may be one as you Father are in me and I in you. I pray that they may be one in us that the world may believe that you sent me." Taking this prayer seriously, Vatican II said the Catholic church should recognize the scandal of separation and undertake the task of reunion. Reunion must be the concern of all Christians. It was not, however, to be Tridentine reunion — return to Rome. The council changed the church's thinking on reunion.

First, it stated that guilt for separation and its effects must be admitted by all Christians. All have shared in the fault for the disunity. Moreover, common guilt requires common forgiveness. Never before had the Catholic church publicly acknowledged its guilt for the division among Christians or asked forgiveness of the Protestant churches. Second, the council said the Christian churches must concentrate on understanding each other. All are responsible for discovering what the churches agree on and share, which is far greater than that which separates them. Sincere efforts must be made to understand the faith commitment of others. All Christians must bring the Christian heritage to bear on the problems of the world. The Christian must become involved with other Christians.

The council issued another reminder on Christian unity. Moving toward reunion requires human effort — for example, recognizing common elements of Christian faith; but this alone will not achieve unity. The effort must be turned over to the Spirit for completion. If unity is achieved, the Spirit will bring it about.

The council's statements on ecumenism, as in many areas, call for action from all Christians. Since all Christians are the church, all share responsibility for unity, not just officials, clergy and theologians. The council's stance on ecumenism is reflected in its language. First, acknowledging that the Catholic church shared guilt for the separation was a dramatic departure. Before this, the Catholic church had not reached out to other Christian churches. As a matter of fact, Protestant churches were rarely referred to as churches. "The church" was the Roman church. In addition, the concentrating on common elements instead of differences, together with the quest for unity in diversity instead of unity in uniformity, were noteworthy steps forward. Theologians and church representatives were given the formal task of finding common ground for moving forward. The ecumenical movement languishes from time to time, but it continues and has had notable successes. The key thing to be kept in mind is that reunion is the common work of all Christians. If Christians cannot see other Christians as brothers and sisters in common faith with one Lord, the scandal remains.

Efforts toward unity are varied. Efforts by the professionals and scholars continue. Some local churches have study groups, shared prayer and worship services. So far the rules prohibit intercommunion, the ultimate sign of shared life, except in limited circumstances. Much needs to be done to awaken the desire for unity and to encourage getting to know each other. Yet, one feels that unity and community are being achieved in common Christian goals and programs. While some Catholics are more open and less arrogant about being in sole possession of the truth, a considerable number have yet to awaken to the need for efforts toward unity. Four centuries of wounds and walls of separation do not give way easily. Christians need to realize the senselessness of separation and accept the mandate to strive for unity. Unfortunately, this awareness is not widespread, nor does it have a high priority with many. Efforts toward unity are at best sporadic. None are worldwide. Perhaps Christians will unite more through common tasks than because their belief, tradition and Lord mandate that they become one church, one people. Yet, unity among Christians would only be a beginning. Still to be addressed would be the large number of non-believers in the world.

Chapter 8

The Future

From the beginning, our thesis has been that to know Christianity, to understand what it means to be a Christian, requires being aware that the belief, worship and practice of Christianity have been shaped by centuries of historical events and culture. In light of that thesis, we must, in conclusion, answer the question, how effective has implementing Vatican II's blueprint been? The best testament to the council's success may be the answer to this question: What does it mean to be a Christian, a Catholic, a people of God, a church in the present century? However future generations may judge Vatican II, it generated a renewed spirit and faced up to the need for examining these vital areas of the church's existence: liturgy, scripture, organization, ministry and the expression of belief. The council's far-reaching scope is itself adequate evidence of the long need to examine the life of the church.

Vatican II is a watershed. We cannot go back to the Tridentine church. How the church will go forward will be determined not by popes, nor clergy, nor the laity alone, but by the shared responsiveness of her people. The council's vision was that all members participate in the life of the church and the Christian mission. Its success will be measured by the degree that all members accept responsibility for working together to accomplish its mandates. The mission of the church after the council will be carried out to the extent that Christians perform what the church is called to do regardless of time, place or culture. This mission is: to be what Jesus is and to do what he does in the world, to bring God's redemptive love to the world. Ultimately, the success of Vatican II will come as Christians work out in their lives the mandates of its documents, not as absolute commands but as a vital dynamic spirit forming the church in history and culture.

What are we to make of the church after Vatican II? To answer, we must keep before us several primary themes that shaped the thought and the documents of the council: the spirit of community, the need for adaptation and change, recapturing the scriptures as the spirit of Christianity, the call to service, and the focus on the church's place in the world. These are the spirit and life of the council. If these permeate the church and its members, the spirit of the council will shape the church of the future.

Sense of community. Concentration on individual Christianity and individual salvation grew out of the Council of Trent. One focused on doing good works to save one's soul, to merit an eternal reward hereafter. Vatican II called upon Christians to realize that Christianity is essentially communitarian; salvation is not an individual affair. One finds and serves Jesus in the community: one is saved as part of a saving community. When realized, this approach will pervade all areas of the church. It will breathe life into collegiality and evangelization. Liturgy will no longer be an occasion for private communing with "my own" God, but a place for being formed together by the word of God and vitalized by the bread of life to serve the world. Community will mean that one does not leave the world to go to God, but goes to the world to bring the gift of God among his people. Christians who understand the spirit of community will see the need for unity among the churches. They will acknowledge that salvation comes through a variety of channels, Christian or not, and that God's saving grace works mysteriously through the world. The spirit of community will remind Christians that the church's mission to teach all nations is for all members, and is not restricted to clergy, religious or missionaries. In this spirit of community, Christians will proclaim the kingdom as Jesus did — a call to witness God's love by manifesting concern for neighbor and the world. Vatican II's spirit of community will remind Christians that faith and salvation are not private possessions, but gifts to be shared to bring new life in Jesus to the world.

Change and renewal. Seeing the church as unchanging is relatively recent, going back to the Council of Trent. Nevertheless, the idea was defended with such vigor that after four centuries only one form of church was recognized as authentic. No wonder that John XXIII's call for a council to reformulate the life of the church was heard with fear and astonishment. It was unthinkable that the church could change its form or the way it expressed its belief. But John and the majority of the council participants decided to face the enormous task of renewing the life of the church and developing forms of church that would be more responsive to the 20th century. Though these forms have not been worked out, renewal and development continue. Many tasks mapped out by the council have yet to be realized. Likewise, implementation of its documents has met with mixed enthusiasm. Despite this, the principle of change and adaptation remains central. This does not mean that the idea of changelessness is no longer a potential stumbling block. Many still look upon change as dangerous to Christian faith. Yet, a growing number of Christians realize that adaptation has been essential to life and growth of the church. True concern has been expressed that if the church does not address the 20th and 21st centuries, it will become relatively insignificant. Those who express this view are committed to deepening the awareness for implementing change.

Foremost on the agenda for change is the manner in which authority is exercised in the church. Centralization and authoritative structure retain a preeminent position. Critics question whether the new code of canon law is in keeping with the spirit of the council. Clearly, collegiality has not made major inroads at the upper levels of administration. The blueprint for change may have been adopted, but fears concerning the primacy of the pope, the teaching authority of the church, and control over orthodoxy still prevail. Nevertheless, a strong segment wants to renew the church. This segment favors the exercise of authority tempered by participation, seeks to balance papal primacy with episcopal collegiality, and sees dissent as necessary in the search for truth.

Prior to Vatican II, the possibility of changing the form in which belief was expressed was unthinkable. Trent accepted the scholastic theological and philosophical language for expressing belief. In the late 19th and early 20th century, the church prohibited exploring contemporary modes of expression. In spite of efforts by outstanding scholars, attempts to find alternative ways of explaining belief and practices remain unacceptable. Though little progress has been made, the efforts go on. Unfortunately, belief and the manner in which it is expressed have become so intertwined that as long as belief cannot change neither can the language. As the end of the 20th century nears, continuing to express faith in scholastic terms becomes more difficult because fewer church leaders and scholars are schooled in it. In addition, with the passage of time, fewer Christians will have studied, worshiped or lived in the church of Trent.

One further thought should be sobering to those who feel that change is not imperative: As history moves on and world cultures and influence change, the world is less dominated by western European and North American culture. The world grows less "Roman" than those who live in the shadow of Rome may care to acknowledge. The church of the Third World — Africa, South and Central America and the Pacific nations — is not of scholastic culture. An understanding of history will make Christians comfortable with adapting expression, structure and worship in a changing world. Openness to change may be as important to implementing the council as working out the blueprint of its documents.

Historical events and needs of the times have shaped the belief and practice of Christianity since Jesus Christ formed his church. Recognizing this reduces the pain, fear and stress in accepting renewal of the church to meet the needs of this century and the next. Education, liturgy, doctrine, language, governance and evangelization all need to be assessed in view of the demands of a changing world, scientific advances, international struggles, newly developing countries, and worldwide crises.

Every age calls for a church to serve that age. Vatican II looks back to the early sources to find what the church did in its origin and to recapture the spirit of those early years; in keeping with the same spirit, it looks to the present to discover ways to solve its problems and meet its needs. Flexibility and adaptation have been constant components of the church's life. To be unwilling to change is to deny what has been a characteristic of the church through all the centuries of her existence. Recognition of the need to address the world in contemporary terms was a driving force of Vatican II.

Scriptural Christianity. The Christian church is the church of Jesus Christ. He is the founder; he is the message; he is the Good News. If the church is to renew, it must do so in keeping with its origins and its mission. This is complicated by the fact that for centuries the church has not had a scriptural orientation in language, liturgy or belief. Catholic scholars were not permitted, until the middle of the 20th century, to use the methods and tools of contemporary biblical scholarship. Since Pius XII's encyclical, *Divino Afflante Spiritu,* scripture scholars have made great strides in understanding the Bible. Unfortunately, little of this has reached the ordinary life of the church. Vatican II forcefully declared that the church would go to its sources and become rooted in the New Testament. The council said the church would do this in all phases of her life: in studying the scriptures for the message intended by the authors, in understanding the faith statements of the early church, in celebrating liturgy that communicates the word of God, and, above all, in coming to know the teaching of Jesus as he lived and preached the kingdom. Scripture is to become the central theme of preaching, especially in the liturgy; likewise, it is to be the core of spirituality and prayer. Vatican II is firm in insisting on restoring scripture to the central place as the source for finding the origin of faith and what it means to lead a Christian life.

Evangelization begins with study of scripture. This includes study of the language, history, purpose and culture of scriptures and use of contemporary scholarship to understand it fully. The insistence on returning to the sources of Christianity is one of the most fruitful of Vatican II's impacts. Jesus' command to his disciples to "go and teach all nations" needs to be implemented primarily with reference to the scriptures, the documents in which Christianity was first formulated and believed. Vatican II returned scripture to the core of Christian life and learning. After many centuries of non-scriptural consciousness, this is one of the council's great gifts.

Service. For too long the church has been thought of in terms of structure, authority, buildings, administration and prayer. All of these are legitimate elements of the church but they do not go to the heart of its mission: to proclaim the Good News. For that mission, all members are equally called to be disciples. Scripture makes this clear in telling us who Jesus was and what he did. The gospel of Mark says: "The Son of Man has come not to be served, but to serve and to give his life in ransom for the many." Therein lies the mission of the disciples: to serve. Christian discipleship is service — meeting whatever needs exist in whatever way possible. The Christian not only worships God and believes in Jesus but lives as Jesus would have one live the life of discipleship. The documents of Vatican II are replete with images of the church and its people as servants. Ministry is service and the role of the primary minister, the pope, is described as the servant of the servants. Where is Christian witness given? How is the kingdom proclaimed? The community of believers gives the answers. It does so in what it says and does inside and outside the community, at home or abroad. The visible sign of Christ is the church. This is why the council refers to the church as sacrament. The church is a people — a living, acting, believing community bringing the message to all persons, across the street or around the world. To be a follower of Jesus is to be concerned for human living and the conditions of life. By council standards, the Christian community must be committed to service, disposing of itself as Jesus did, providing support, ministering, healing, teaching, consoling, correcting, providing spiritual leadership, and, in general, spending its talents for others. It should not be surprising to find the Christian concerned with poverty, peace, nuclear armaments, disease, deprivation, human rights, the aged, the neglected, the needy, the untaught, the unrepentant. Life in Jesus means building the kingdom on earth, living for others as Jesus did, while remembering that it cost him life itself. The spirit of the Vatican II church is a spirit of service. It is a spirit remembering that Jesus made clear what he considered the mark of his servants: "Come, you have my Father's blessing. . . . For I was hungry and you gave me food, I was thirsty and you gave me drink, I was a stranger and you welcomed me, naked and you clothed me. I was ill and you comforted me, in prison and you came to visit me. . . . As often as you did it for one of my least, you did it for me." Service in the kingdom is not a new call, but one that Vatican II recalls and holds before us as a reminder of what it is to be a church, a people of God.

Church in the world. Much needs to be done to bring about the reality envisioned and outlined in Vatican II. Prior to the council, the church looked upon itself as set aside from the world; a Christian left the world to work in and for the church. The world was viewed as material, sinful, opposed to Christian values and life; it was a hostile, alien place. Spirituality denied this world as home. We were strangers and transients. Christians were told to look to heaven as the place to be; the kingdom of God would come in the next life. Goodness was highly individualistic, and actions were carefully weighed as they related to winning heaven and eternal salvation.

The Vatican II document treating relationships with the world and its affairs is entitled *The Church in the Modern World.* Note that the title is not the church *and* the world, nor the church *against* the world. The document urges Christians to address the dynamic reality of life in the world — a mixture of goodness and sinfulness. It urges Christians to act as leaven to renew the world in Christ. The church relates to and interacts with the world. No area of life is outside the Christian's concern. Witness to the gospel occurs only in interaction with human activity in the world. Even though this activity includes evil — injustice, persecution and corruption of values — the world, nevertheless, remains the place of God's creative love.

Vatican II challenges all Christians to enter more fully into the world because that is where human life undergoes change and formation, and customs, beliefs and values are sustained. In each generation, Christians create God's kingdom in the events of history and culture. Jesus did not pray to the Father that he take the disciples out of the world, only that he guard them from evil. Vatican II's spirit of Christian community is directed toward the world. There is no other place to proclaim the Good News of salvation. If the Christian community is to offer its message, it must be firmly rooted in the world. Christians must be involved in family, social institutions, historic and political events, education, work and play, birth and death, life and sickness, healing and consoling, entertainment and business. Withdrawal cannot be service or witness. The Christian in the world and the mission of the church to serve go hand in hand. The rediscovery of this is Vatican II's legacy.

Applying its own spirit and vision, Vatican II is both an event in time and a continuing process. Were we to stop at a given point and say, "Now, there, that's finished," we would be undermining the purpose of Vatican II. Some say another council, or two or three, are needed to work out the details of Vatican II. True, many steps toward renewal seem faltering. Yet, no council make things happen according to its mandate. Renewal is the task of the entire church, requiring participation by all members because it is such a momentous undertaking. If in the spirit of the council Christians come to understand that history is change and development, renewal will never come to an end. Adaptation will continue as each generation responds to the needs of its time.

The worst error would be to think that opening a window and drawing a blueprint means that by some miracle Vatican II's spirit and documents will be quickly perfected. Therein lies the absolutizing of another single form of church.

A sense of history means an awareness of the fact that a church built to serve one age is not apt to be able to serve another. It must forever reform and renew itself. A sense of history also means that if the church is to realize what is essential to Christianity, it must steep itself in Christianity's original documents, the New Testament scriptures. The church must discover what being a Christian meant to the early church, which wrote those scriptures. Only then can the church take that understanding and recreate the same kind of church for today. Only then can it build a church whose structure and spirit express the Christianity characteristic of the first church. If the church does not know that Christianity in essence is community, it does not know Christianity. To the degree that all members find and serve Jesus in community the church is the true Christian church, the people of God.

This, then, is the work of Vatican II and the work to be accomplished after Vatican II. We must not think that the work can be completed and all the documents implemented. That would be a final error and a new absolute. That is not what an awareness of history tells us about life in the church and in the kingdom.